Little Fauss and Big Halsy

Little Fauss
and Big Halsy

A SCREENPLAY BY
Charles Eastman

FARRAR, STRAUS AND GIROUX
NEW YORK

This is the original screenplay upon which the motion picture *Little Fauss and Big Halsy* is based. It is not the final shooting script.

CREDITS

WRITTEN BY: *Charles Eastman*
PRODUCED BY: *Albert S. Ruddy*
DIRECTED BY: *Sidney J. Furie*
ASSOCIATE PRODUCER: *Gray Frederickson*
EXECUTIVE PRODUCER: *Brad Dexter*
DIRECTOR OF PHOTOGRAPHY: *Ralph Woolsey, A.S.C.*
ART DIRECTION: *Larry Paull*
SET DECORATION: *Audrey Blasdell*
EDITED BY: *Argyle Nelson, Jr.*
PRODUCTION MANAGER: *Terry Morse, Jr.*
SONGS AND INSTRUMENTAL MUSIC PERFORMED
  AND SUPERVISED BY: *Johnny Cash*

CAST

HALSY KNOX: *Robert Redford*
LITTLE FAUSS: *Michael J. Pollard*
RITA NEBRASKA: *Lauren Hutton*
SEALLY FAUSS: *Noah Beery*
"MOM" FAUSS: *Lucille Benson*
THE PHOTOGRAPHER: *Ray Ballard*
MONETH: *Linda Gaye Scott*
SYLVENE MCFALL: *Erin O'Reilly*
RICK NIFTY: *Ben Archibeck*

Little Fauss and Big Halsy was produced by Alfran Productions, Inc., and Furie Productions, Inc. It is distributed by Paramount Pictures.

Little Fauss and Big Halsy

Country Road, Southwest U.S.A.

Nothing could be more at peace nor remoter from human-kind than this bend in a country road. Everything describes a lazy afternoon buzzing warmly.

Suddenly from beyond the rise and preceding the sound it creates comes a racing motorcycle sinisterly manned by a helmeted, leathered, numbered form, and following shortly come two or three more of this sort.

We are on the back turn of a small country hare scrambles course; that is, a road somewhere in New Mexico or Arizona converted to this use.

At relentless intervals, trailing riders bombard the scene with gravel, grit and roar, each twisting vigorously to maneuver the turn, and some all but drift off the track before they recover a straightaway.

The dust has almost settled again when a lone straggler appears like an afterthought. The sound of his single motor, puny in the backwash of silence, speaks low of this activity on a drowsy Sunday and seems to say that man is diminished by his machines.

Certainly this man is. His standing in the race already hopeless, he now takes a turn for the worse and loses his bike. It slides from under him as he leans into the curve. Almost comically, he is propelled forward on his feet several yards before he can come to a stop.

Dazed but indomitable, he returns to his vehicle on a run and rights it hurriedly. In the effort, however, his helmet falls off, to reveal sweat-drenched hair and thick glasses and a young man of twenty we will come to know as LITTLE FAUSS. Blushing as though there were witnesses to this confusion, he returns the helmet to his head and regains the track with his bike, though not without another goofy moment during which he reflects on the correct direction to take to avoid head-on collision with his colleagues.

Then he proceeds, wagging his rear suspension eagerly.

Straightaway

Bordering the straightaway on the one hand is an incline roped off for spectators and on the other a gully roped off for the pits, the latter more heavily-peopled and outnumbering the audience opposite.

Though rather spread out by now, the main contingent of cycles descends this worn avenue one after the other in speeds which for all the crouched effort and concentration of the riders fail somehow to justify the urgent fixity of attention given by the tuners, buddies, fathers, and small-time sponsors from the pits.

4

And the Pits

It is here, in the face of the permanently smudged, adoring devotee who pursues his racer down the track and around the turn with squinted reverence, that the undeniable drama of the race takes place. These satellites are desperately if incredibly involved, and now as their racers pass they run to another section of track, not to miss a moment of what to the outsider seems an unchanging routine of controlled speed; and some hold up slates and pieces of cardboard on which the laps accomplished are announced to the cycled saviors in transit and their positions proclaimed.

Straightaway

And because of this action the straggler LITTLE FAUSS appears and passes the pits with no eyes on him and alone on the straightaway his limited velocity suggests someone playing the clown. We detect an embarrassed side glance to the spectators as he goes by which apologizes for this ultimate position but does not regret the limelight, faint and fading as it is.

Seally's Sanitation

At the top of the bank of spectators overlooking the straightaway are two homemade narrow booths with slightly askew doors. One is marked *MEN* and the other *WOMAN*, and printed on the side of each in the same unsteady hand is this trademark: *Seally's Sanitation*. Folks of different sizes and shapes are divided by gender into two long lines before these booths, and some as they wait stare down the bank at the distant sputter and grind of the scrambles.

SEALLY FAUSS, whom we notice because he is not in line and also because he wears thick glasses identical to his son's, regards the tardy figure of LITTLE rounding the straightaway curve below.

> SEALLY
> That's the son-of-a-gun you ought to get a picture of.

In the line extending from *MEN*, one person only is not turned toward the race, and that is a PHOTOGRAPHER whose superabundance of equipment marks him as an amateur; he intends to reload his camera in the shade of the toilet and is impatient to do so before the finish of the race.

> PHOTOGRAPHER
> What lap is it?

> SEALLY
> He gets a chance to race enough one of them factories pick him up like *that*.

The PHOTOGRAPHER obliges the bumpkin with a disinterested glance to the track.

> PHOTOGRAPHER
> He's last, isn't he?

> SEALLY
> Don't nobody know sickles like Little.

The PHOTOGRAPHER returns to his camera.

PHOTOGRAPHER
(*Preoccupied*) How many laps left?

SEALLY
Don't get no time *on* his bike though, 'cept Sundays.
And then he's half the time off.

And he likewise returns to business and with no small
pride surveys the masses waiting at his doors.

SEALLY
But he's got to work. Like the rest of us.

PHOTOGRAPHER
These your facilities?

SEALLY
Shoot, yeah! Got my hands full today!

PHOTOGRAPHER
(*Making conversation*) Well, like the man
says . . . build a better mousetrap.

SEALLY
(*Self-important*) You get a crowd like this together
and people don't stop to realize all the problems
come to a head.

PHOTOGRAPHER
That's people for you . . .

SEALLY
Sanitation alone is staggering!

PHOTOGRAPHER
All they want to do is turn the other cheek.

The Track

Flagmen along the route study the racers as they pass:

Old men with surreptitious cans of beer handy in a nearby bush;

Middle-aged boosters in loafers and comic golf hats;

Puffed-up, pocky, gray-skinned youths with blemished belts of belly oozing out between their Levi's and their swarthy t-shirts.

All members of the Columbine Motorcycle Club, these officials and lookouts wear bright brief silks so stating. And bundled against the breeze and getting too much sun, an appropriate assortment of women, official and aloof, accompany them on stones and logs and folding chairs. And here and there untended kids run, significantly unimpressed by that adult toy the motorcycle, and fabricate other adventure in weeds and rocks and trees surrounding.

In visiting these posts, we have covered the more dramatic turns, ramps and plunges of the track.

The Toilet

The PHOTOGRAPHER holds his breath sickly in the gassy gloom of the toilet. Outside, the congested roar of several bikes on the straightaway and some crowd reaction pressure him to hurry the procedure of reloading his camera and this compounds his awkwardness in the small space and the all but strangling effect of his equipment. He grinds his teeth as he works and curses tightly.

Then something in the nature of a sudden stillness outside much like a huge general intake of breath causes him to stop and listen, and this moment is followed by the garbled alarm and excitement of the race announcer over the public address.

The PHOTOGRAPHER pushes open the toilet door.

The Grounds

No one is waiting outside the toilets now. There has been an accident and people run toward the turn that concludes the straightaway.

Already the PHOTOGRAPHER is running also.

Those not drawn to blood collect in downcast huddles to wait out a felt but unexpressed dismay.

SEALLY FAUSS, who might have cause to fear, conceals concern by closing the toilet door. Then he scans the opposite direction, with gaunt hope that LITTLE still trails.

The ambulance crawls seriously forward, its red eye blinking your money's worth of disaster while the public address remarks politely that indeed the game is rough and tumble and then attempts to transfer the general attention back to the competition, which continues.

Straightaway Turn

Officials, hysterical efficiency experts, butters-in and sa-maritans flag the racers around the scene of the accident and otherwise direct operations as the ambulance backs in for a convenient pickup.

"You go along with him in the ambulance." "Where are his car keys?" "I got his bike." "Where you parked, Ted?" "He's broke his back."

The victim is conscious, if not altogether bright-eyed. He lies on his side in a fetal position. He hands up his car keys but refuses to be straightened out as the ambulance attendants attempt to get him onto a stretcher. They slide a board under his hips as though he was something spilled and without handles, and only in this way can they get him up.

Over him, his wife stands weeping in a strangely shallow, distracted, extraneous, almost disinterested manner, as though grief were an obligation already exhausted. Somebody find the kids, she says as they seal her into the ambulance with the husband she will not look at under these circumstances.

The ambulance moves slowly, then must stop. It waits for a break in the cycle traffic to get across the track and on with its moody mission.

And even now, despite this heavy moment, a wild-haired woman standing trackside crouches down and whips one arm out in a broad gesture of encouragement to her man as he bullets by: disaster to one is good fortune to another.

The Grounds

The PHOTOGRAPHER climbs back up the slope toward an aluminum lunch wagon marked *Mom's Chow,* before which a pudgy woman plaintively eats a sandwich and waits details of the wreck. Her thick glasses and the familiar inexpert printing of her sign at once identify her as another Fauss.

MOM

Hurt pretty bad?

PHOTOGRAPHER

I don't know. Somebody said broke his back.

MOM

My my, how'd he do that?

Behind them, casually stealing a couple of sandwiches, is a shirtless, shiftless satyr we will come to know as HALSY KNOX.

HALSY

How'd he do *that?*

Sandwiches safely secreted in a helmet he swings like a purse, he passes between them, aghast but disengaged.

HALSY

Cycles is a mean toy, lady.

And shaking his head with an easy chagrin born of bronze nakedness and plenty of beer, he descends the slope, lithe and athletic, amid the leathered and Levi'd overweight of his brothers and sisters.

Reverse Angle

While MOM FAUSS gives change to a customer from a coin dispenser she wears on her belt, the PHOTOGRAPHER lifts his camera to his eye and studies HALSY's retreat down the shale and scrub of the incline.

View through Telephoto Lens

The focus sharpens from the fuzzy flesh of HALSY's bare back to the grotesque draftsmanship of an eloquent scar that descends the length of his well-tanned spine.

> MOM
> (*Voice over*) Just taking pictures for yourself or what?

> PHOTOGRAPHER
> (*Voice over*) Did you see that guy's back?

But pelvis, hips and chest are examined just as closely, and finally HALSY's face, cupped beneath an upside-down sailor hat, strong and self-approving and endowed with the standard magic of comic-book good looks.

> MOM
> (*Voice over*) I'll tell you who you should get a picture of.

HALSY shoots a contemptuous kiss at the PHOTOGRAPHER who cruises him.

The Grounds

To cover his discomfort at HALSY's gesture, the PHOTO-GRAPHER lowers his camera and pretends to have some trouble with the lens.

> MOM
> I'll pay you if it comes out.

> PHOTOGRAPHER
> Damn dumb thing's jammed.

Take your time.

She checks the distant stretches of the track.

MOM

He won't be in for quite a spell.

PHOTOGRAPHER

Who's that?

He lifts his camera again and as though it were binoculars he scans the slopes urgently.

MOM

You let Little look at it. If it's broke, he'll fix it good.

PHOTOGRAPHER

You see where that guy went?

MOM

Comes to anything mechanical and Little's all but eerie.

Backcountry

But LITTLE's bike has quit him and buzzards circle overhead.

He looks up, stinging sweat spilling into his eyes, and if he were more revealing of his feelings, one would see he considered such gloomy company as the buzzards only just in view of his poor performance. But as his face is subject to no more expression than a squint, all that meets the eye is a pattern of moist dirt on

13

his cheeks and flat hair at his temples curled into ringlets by sweat. And further, since he is neither short nor diminutive in any way except for some rather engaging mannerisms of approximate blindness, it becomes evident that the name LITTLE is given and not descriptive.

Helmet cradled in one arm, he pushes his heavy machine through the hot brush and boulders that line the track, threatened loudly now and then by those still in the race.

Slope

HALSY tends to statuesque poses, especially when he wears no shirt and sports the inverted sailor hat that keeps his nose from burning. It is not that he is so good-looking but that he advertises, and in a world gone to pot, slenderness is power.

He stands now beside a disgruntled dumpling of a GIRL who sits on the ground at his feet and has had nothing better from him in the entire two weeks of their relationship; yet if the steam of her boredom is any sign, she belongs to him completely and has no other resource.

HALSY belongs to no one. Sleek, scarred, he munches the last of his stolen sandwiches and watches the race with a relaxed precision that seems to see more than there is there.

GIRL

(*Grumping*) Where'd you get that?

He drops the helmet into her lap.

HALSY

Bought it.

GIRL

Like heck. With what?

HALSY

It was hanging on a tree outside the terlet.

GIRL

So you just helped yourself?

HALSY

If it wasn't me, it'd be somebody.

GIRL

Is that supposed to be supper?

He hands her the remaining crusts of bread as the flagman proclaims the final lap with yellow pennant.

The GIRL would like to decline these crumbs in favor of a square meal, but hunger rules out such airs and she eats gratefully in spite of herself.

Final Lap

The action of the final lap as studied by the lofty HALSY from the slope;

The grimy LITTLE from somewhere in the entrails of the track;

And the PHOTOGRAPHER, who covers this unspectacular and poorly attended finish, wherein - the flagman seems rather self-important and overstylish for such a primitive event.

Afterwards

Spectators flow across the track and into the pits, where blackened racers glide home surrounded by beer-bearing disciples; other spectators crawl across the slope toward their cars and cars ascend the rutty roads toward the sunset.

Decibel by decibel the sound one has become accustomed to diminishes from a roar to a final plaintive putter and then to silence.

The WINNER abandons his bike almost immediately in a spirit more of quitting time than of triumph and zipping down his leathers he rushes to a small wall, behind which he quickly changes to other clothes. One would suppose by his hurry that he had a date; certainly winning took nothing special, nor gave it, since he led all the way.

Divested of his leathers and helmet, this is just a bony kid, and clustered around him in taunting praise are others of his ilk, poorly-complexioned and stringy-haired. And shortly they are joined by more racers, who also strip rapidly to baggy underwear and slumping socks, as though to relieve themselves of the burden of advertising. But alas even their t-shirts proclaim some sponsorship and one suspects morbidly that the frequent tattoo bruised into the sallow skin is also a trade name or bike-shop affiliation.

RACER 1

You may of sold a bunch of Contraltos, Ackerman, but the draft board still got you, ha ha ha.

LITTLE arrives straddling his bike and walking it, leaning over and listening to its faint heartbeat.

WINNER (ACKERMAN)

I told you to condense your sledge flux, Little.
I got the same deal.

LITTLE rises, blinking.

LITTLE

I was going as fast as I ever went in my whole
life and then I fell off.

WINNER

You coming to Mendoza?

LITTLE

Maybe I better unblow my flange anchor or
something.

And he leans down over his bike again and continues on.

RACER 2

What's going on at Mendoza?

RACER 1

Beer's on Ackerman because he's going to Veetnom.

We *pan* with LITTLE through the pits as he approaches
SEALLY and MOM and the all but captive PHOTOGRAPHER.

SEALLY

Thought the buzzards had gone and got you.

MOM

Did you see me waving?

LITTLE

I was going as fast as I ever had went in my whole
life and then I fell off.

SEALLY

You go too fast. If you'd stay on, you'd win.

17

MOM

Did you break your bike?

LITTLE

I broke my bike.

SEALLY

That's how you win. You stay on.

LITTLE squints at the elaborate camera, at the same time
ignoring the PHOTOGRAPHER.

LITTLE

What's that? Movies?

To set them up for the shot, MOM pulls on the PHOTOG-
RAPHER and pushes LITTLE into place.

MOM

Come on, Seally. Hurry up.

But SEALLY holds back, wincing formidably.

SEALLY

I can't. I got gas.

MOM

Get your ass over here.

LITTLE holds her off.

LITTLE

Just me and my bike okay?

MOM

(*Mock hurt*) Well, touché for you. (*To* SEALLY)
Never mind, pop. (*To* LITTLE) I just wanted one so
we could see how dirty your face is anyway.

SEALLY

Don't bother the man, dopey.

MOM

I told him we'd pay him if anything turns out.

SEALLY

(*To* PHOTOGRAPHER) What do you think of a boy, anyway, who sleeps with his own motorcycle in his room?

MOM

Just one for the mantel is all I want. We haven't got a picture on the whole mantelpiece, Seal.

SEALLY

What is it, one of them instant things?

PHOTOGRAPHER

(*Dim promise*) I'll get your address.

Having found at last what seems a worthwhile angle, the PHOTOGRAPHER snaps a picture of LITTLE stiff and posey against the mellow light of the setting sun.

Overcome by this beauty, MOM takes SEALLY's arm.

MOM

(*Sniffing*) Life is too short, darn it.

SEALLY

Somebody's had herself a beer.

MOM

Goes by just too damn fast.

LITTLE

Just like me, huh?

MOM

You hold still.

PHOTOGRAPHER

I'm all done.

LITTLE

I was going by so fast as I had ever went in my whole life and then I—

The PHOTOGRAPHER is retreating.

MOM

Give the man our address, dopey.

PHOTOGRAPHER

I can get it off your facilities.

SEALLY

No, by all means take my card.

MOM

I always tell him the day he starts bringing his work home with him is the day I move out.

And she wags her hand before her face to dispel imaginary odors.

SEALLY winces again for good measure as he hands the PHOTOGRAPHER his card.

SEALLY

No, sir, you can laugh but I haven't had a good stool since I got into Portable Potties and that's a fact.

The PHOTOGRAPHER examines the card with disbelieving distaste.

PHOTOGRAPHER
Portable Potties?

SEALLY

P.P. Get it? She come up with that.

MOM

Seally Fauss, I did not!

LITTLE

I was going as fast as I had ever went in my whole entire life today.

SEALLY

Yeah, but you fell off.

LITTLE

Yeah, I fell off.

SEALLY

You want to stay on, son.

MOM

(*Calling after the* PHOTOGRAPHER) We'll be glad to pay if any's any good.

Portable Potties

Evening has descended and the raceway is all but deserted now, though in the distance we see a dilapidated pickup truck, and approaching from this direction, the still shirtless HALSY.

In the foreground, a truck trailer bearing the legend *Portable Potties* is hitched to *Mom's Chow* catering wagon, and the combined strength of the three Fausses is at work pushing and pulling the ramshackle toilets up a ramp and on board.

HALSY's arrival at the trailer coincides with a major effort on the part of the Fauss family to load their truck. It doesn't occur to him, however, to give them a hand.

> HALSY
> How about you guys giving me a push, okay?

> SEALLY
> (*Straining*) We're a mite busy ourselves, mister.

> HALSY
> Oh hell sure. Take your time.

And he shuffles picturesquely to an at-ease posture.

As they continue their labors unaided, MOM responds to the indolent, almost arrogant HALSY with uneasy distrust, while SEALLY openly registers dislike. Though he is over twenty and his own man, LITTLE habitually lets his parents deal with strangers and other difficulties and so he ignores HALSY as a matter of course.

> HALSY
> Me and the wife come over from Mendoza, the dang thing cutting out on me every five minutes. And now the dang thing won't even start and my wife's getting hotter'n hell.

He indicates his pathetic companion leaning against the dingy pickup in the distance, and we see that her mood is anything but wifely, righteous or hotter'n hell, but as yet we don't suspect that HALSY lies and loads the moment and steals and cheats as casually as he breathes.

He has no wife or any other thing but the pickup and the motorcycle it carries and his wits. Least of all has he any spine, and that is perhaps why he holds himself so stiff and upright.

To compensate for SEALLY's coolness, LITTLE and MOM oblige the stranger with a look toward his little woman and while they work respond faintly to his dauntless if needful good nature.

> HALSY
> She's expecting a steak dinner and I said, honey, cool down, them folks over there won't think nothing of giving us a little push.

The toilets are on board and, tense and angry, SEALLY secures them tightly with rope.

> HALSY
> Got all your beer locked up?

> MOM
> I don't sell no beer.

> HALSY
> Not licensed, huh?

SEALLY jumps down from the trailer.

> SEALLY
> Load up your bike, Little.

> HALSY
> Damn it all, I'd like to buy you all a beer.

But SEALLY proceeds unresponsive around to the cabin of the catering wagon, MOM following.

SEALLY

(*Mumbling*) Monkey-faced Sideburns!

MOM

Don't get riled, Seally.

SEALLY

Go to hell with all his flair, for all I care.

MOM

They'll be stranded.

SEALLY

I'm not giving no hand to no undesirables, Mom!

He climbs into the driver's seat as MOM goes around the front of the wagon to the passenger's side.

Meanwhile, in back LITTLE pushes his heavy bike up the ramp and onto the trailer.

HALSY

Hey, do you got a cigarette?

LITTLE

Don't smoke.

HALSY

I just gave away my last cigarette.

And he taps his bare chest abstractly where once there was a pocket and perhaps cigarettes.

HALSY

Spent my last two bucks to get here today, damnit.

Need has created some nervousness, and SEALLY's disregard has pushed HALSY into desperate straits.

24

HALSY

Blew my pickup getting over here and then burned out my bike in the trials, so I didn't win nothing. And lost my sponsor I could of had if I'd had any luck and now I don't even have a smoke.

The bike is loaded and secured.

SEALLY

(*Calling from up front*) You ready, son?

LITTLE

(*Calling back*) This guy wants a push, Dad.

The trailer gives a lurch and LITTLE grabs on as SEALLY starts the truck.

HALSY

If I can just get a little shove, it'll start right off.

He takes a few trusting steps after the now moving truck and trailer but he is quickly left behind.

HALSY

What the hell damnit, I need a push!

On the back of the trailer, LITTLE shrugs in a faint gesture that is some part apology for strong-willed parents and some part sympathy for hungry wives and burned-out engines but is in no part involved, and HALSY shrinks as distance grows between them.

Wagon Cab Interior

MOM and SEALLY bump over the uneven ground, SEALLY fuming.

25

MOM

Sideburns don't necessarily mean bum, Dad. Your own dad was a bearded man, as I recall.

SEALLY

That was then. This is now.

MOM

You're going to have yourself a gastric fit.

SEALLY

Long as I'm in it I'm going to protect the name of motorcycles, Mom, and any undesirables come around with earrings in their nose is going to have me to contend with.

MOM

That boy had no earring in his nose, dopey.

SEALLY belches lengthily.

MOM

Now see what I mean?

SEALLY

(*Worried*) I'm going to lose that burrito.

MOM

And all over a undesirable is what gets me. Where's the sense in that?

SEALLY

Worth it, if it keeps cycling clean.

MOM

Not to me, if you're going to be on the pot all night.

Slope

HALSY returns up the slope toward his worn and dusty pickup, his numbered bike in back. The GIRL waits for him.

> GIRL
> Now what?

He leans against the fender beside her and sighs, surveying the barren landscape shadowed now and suddenly cool and sibilant in the approach of night.

> GIRL
> Want your shirt?

He sights the PHOTOGRAPHER packing his equipment into the trunk of a sportscar. An unlikely source of help, considering the disparity in size between their vehicles, but all there is left for HALSY to try.

> GIRL
> What are you going to do?

Highway

It is night and the truck and trailer move at a steady clip down the highway.

Trailer

LITTLE lies on the floor of the trailer looking up at the stars through gleaming spokes and handlebars and tubes and wiring. He is all but under his bike. One hand holds the warm rubber of the front tire and absently strokes it with loving thumb; one leg is cocked between the wheels and pulls the rear tire affectionately to his groin.

Suddenly his emotion can be contained no longer and all his arms and legs encircle and enfold the noble bike and a squeal of urgent pleasure takes on the wind.

Mendoza Roadhouse Interior

The WINNER, ACKERMAN, sits at the bar with RACERS 1 and 2. They are picking their cheeks and reliving the race, as HALSY pushes through with three empty beer bottles.

> HALSY
>
> Really working today, huh? Cranking around those corners with the big boys.

He puts the bottles on the bar and indicates a repeat to the bartender.

As the WINNER and his friends don't know HALSY, this intrusion is dampening.

> WINNER
>
> You race today?

> HALSY
>
> On that dumb-ass course? Not me, buddy.

> WINNER
>
> I didn't think I seen ya.

> HALSY
>
> Youd'a seen me, babe. I'd'a had you to the fence.

> WINNER
>
> What class you race?

HALSY takes three fresh beers from the bartender.

> HALSY
>
> Put that on the dinner tab, would you. My manager's got it.

He departs to the booths across the room.

> WINNER
>
> Who the hell's that?

> RACER 1
>
> That's that cat got suspended out at Cascade for booze in the pits, I think.

> WINNER
>
> Wow, that's a whole season, man.

> RACER 1
>
> Rides pretty good, too.

> WINNER
>
> Better had, the way he talks.

Booth

HALSY sits down with new beer for himself, for the GIRL, who eats with shamed concentration, and for the PHOTOGRAPHER, who is a little uneasy and excessive in the flush of a new-found friendship.

> HALSY
>
> Let's see now, where was I at?

> PHOTOGRAPHER
>
> You were going to tell me how you broke your spine, which is what first caught my eye.

HALSY

You know I can't sleep in a bed to this day?

PHOTOGRAPHER

Good grief, where do you sleep? On the floor?

HALSY

That's right, that's where. On the floor.

The PHOTOGRAPHER puts a solicitous arm around the GIRL's shoulders.

PHOTOGRAPHER

That must make it pretty hard on the little lady.

GIRL

What?

PHOTOGRAPHER

If your husband's on the floor all night, what I'm saying is, it must be pretty hard on you.

GIRL

Him?

PHOTOGRAPHER

It would on me.

He removes his arm.

GIRL

I haven't even seen a floor since I met him, much less a bed.

HALSY

We been sleeping in the car.

And he pulls her into a one-armed embrace.

PHOTOGRAPHER
You're not married, then?

HALSY
She's my buddy, my bosom buddy. Aren't you, honey? Show him your bosoms.

PHOTOGRAPHER
(*Taking the plunge*) Well then, why don't I just get a room out here then and we all just settle down for the night.

HALSY extends his hand.

HALSY
My name's Halsy Knox, and this here's what's her name from Simi.

PHOTOGRAPHER
How do you do. Sylvene McFall.

HALSY
(*Agreeing*) We're all just free, white and twenty-one, I guess.

PHOTOGRAPHER
That's right. And anything goes?

The PHOTOGRAPHER is slow to release HALSY's hand until the terms of the bargain are clear, and the GIRL, anticipating nervously her responsibilities in this transaction, claims HALSY's free arm for what security is there, which isn't much.

GIRL
(*Trying to be bright*) We've slept just about anywhere but on a mattress, him and me, the whole two weeks we been in love.

Motel Room Interior

In the murky light of early dawn the scrambled naked arms and legs of two men and a woman are just visible amid the sheets of a large double bed. One recognizes HALSY's scar, and shortly this back begins to stir.

Awake now and aware of his surroundings HALSY extricates himself from his bedfellows, the GIRL and the PHOTOGRAPHER, and stands apart; then in cautious quiet he puts his clothes on.

Dressed except for his shoes, he goes through the PHOTOGRAPHER's pants in search of the man's wallet and, finding it, removes what money there is left.

Shoes in hand, he tiptoes to the door and from there looks back at the human debris he leaves behind. He spots the camera and returns for it, putting it around his neck before he exits.

> GIRL
> (*Still half asleep*) Honey?

Motel Exterior

The pickup moves quickly out the driveway of *The Nook Motel*.

Highway Day

The pickup speeds down the highway.

> HALSY
> (*Voice over*) Dear *Cycle Life* . . .

32

Pickup Interior

Affluent and unencumbered, HALSY faces the road ahead with confidence and enthusiasm.

HALSY

(*Voice over*) How would you guys like a eye-witness story of a guy's travels all through South America and all his adventures in a foreign country on a bike? I think the readers of *Cycle Life* would really go for that, with pictures took by a professional camera which I already got. Please send me a tape recorder to record my thoughts and a hundred dollars a week to include expenses.

Street

The pickup cruises down the central street of a small town and stops before a cycle shop.

HALSY

(*Voice over*) P.S. I would also consider traveling and writing tales of adventure in Hawaii, Europe and Africa.

Cycle-Shop Interior

LITTLE is behind the parts counter as HALSY enters. They recognize each other but without comment or acknowledgment.

HALSY

Got any bore bafflers for a Contralto 450?

LITTLE wags his head in a negative so hopeless it is almost undiscernible.

> HALSY
>
> No?

> LITTLE
>
> No got.

> HALSY
>
> Shit.

> LITTLE
>
> Could get 'em maybe in a week.

> HALSY
>
> What about a risi gusset?

> LITTLE
>
> Risi gussets we got.

He disappears briefly into the stalls behind the counter. HALSY whistles loudly and taps his fingers as though to attract the attention of anyone else in the shop. LITTLE comes back with a small gadget in a plastic bag. HALSY tears open the bag and examines the part closely.

> LITTLE
>
> It's brang new. What are you looking at? It's perfect.

> HALSY
>
> Some kind of groove or something scratched on the inside.

LITTLE takes the part and, removing his glasses, inspects it closely.

HALSY

Owner here?

LITTLE

Can't hurt nothing if it's on the inside.

HALSY

Give me another one.

LITTLE puts his glasses back on and departs philosophically to get a fresh gusset. HALSY again taps and whistles broadly, and when LITTLE returns this time, he does not examine the item heretofore so questionable.

HALSY

Thought maybe I'd promote myself a couple tires if the boss is around.

LITTLE takes an order form to write up the gusset, and that is the extent of his reaction.

HALSY

Them I got seen too many races. If I head out to the desert Sunday. You going?

LITTLE continues to make out the bill.

HALSY

You got any say-so around here?

LITTLE shakes his head in another imperceptible no.

HALSY

Or hell, you probably do all the promotion racing around here anyway, right?

LITTLE

That's a buck fifty-nine for the gusset.

HALSY

You got all the deal sewed up, huh?

LITTLE

He'll be back after lunch, if you want to see the boss. Otherwise I ain't authorized for nothing.

HALSY

No hell, buddy, if you're his rider I wouldn't move in on you.

He pockets the as yet unpaid-for gusset.

HALSY

Hell, my contract with Contralto wouldn't let me ride for any boondock dealer anyway. Just wanted to see what the feeling was.

LITTLE

That's a buck fifty-nine, by the way, for the gusset.

HALSY

Oh, yeah. By the way, can I bum the use of your bore compressor for five minutes?

This, in spite of the large sign over the counter stating: *No Tools Loaned Without Mechanic Charges.*

LITTLE indicates the sign, though it could not have been missed.

HALSY

Yeah, but the boss ain't here now.

LITTLE

He could come back.

HALSY

After lunch, you said.

Cycle Lot and Garage Exterior

HALSY backs his pickup into place and unloads his bike from the back. LITTLE observes him from the parts counter and then comes out, gusset bill in hand.

> LITTLE
>
> If you're contracted, how come Contralto don't take better care of you?

> HALSY
>
> Hell with Contralto, man. Contralto can go to hell. You know what they done? I quit 'em.

> LITTLE
>
> Yeah, but you win a hundred percent then. You don't have to split with no mechanic.

> HALSY
>
> Just give me my own bike and my own know-how and leave me alone. Do you have a loose lefty?

LITTLE goes for the tool and returns with it.

> HALSY
>
> Except now if I want to race it's got to be scrambles and hares. At least until my contract runs out.

> LITTLE
>
> Oh yeah, that's right incidentally risi gussets are a buck-fifty and, let's see, nine cents tax.

HALSY drops what he is doing and reaching into his pocket expels a giant sigh.

> HALSY
>
> You sure got some small-time ideas about friendship, man.

LITTLE

You mean about last night?

HALSY

How much is tax?

LITTLE

My dad's got stomach disodor.

HALSY

No, I mean about right now. Do you think I'm
not going to pay you, or what?

LITTLE

No, heck, forget it.

HALSY

No, I pay my bills, man.

LITTLE

If you're going to use a gusset, you better face
it first.

And he crouches down by the bike.

HALSY

Face it?

LITTLE

If you don't want any lick stress.

HALSY

I'm no scientist. I just ride bikes.

And he surrenders the tools to LITTLE, who claims them
eagerly.

LITTLE

You sponsored guys sure don't know beans about
bikes, that's one thing.

HALSY

Yeah, you get spoiled . . .

He heads for a coffee dispenser and cups.

HALSY

This coffee for the general use?

LITTLE

Customers.

HALSY fills his cup.

HALSY

These sponsored guys are a pain in the ass anyway.
I hate 'em. Any sugar?

LITTLE leaves work on the bike and crosses to the
coffee urn, wiping greasy hands on a rag and sighing
in overstated patience.

HALSY

Don't have to stay up all night working on a
bike the night before, but can stay up all night
just loving the women and drinking it up and
whatever they damn want.

LITTLE

Where's your wife this morning?

HALSY

My who?

LITTLE presents HALSY with cream and sugar.

LITTLE

I'm not your wife, you know.

HALSY

Oh yeah, that's right, she's a stewardess.

He fills his cup with all the cream and sugar it will hold.

> HALSY
>
> Had a early flight out this morning, so I didn't get no breakfast.

Then referring to a piece of doughnut by the coffee urn:

> HALSY
>
> Whose doughnut is this? Is this somebody's?

LITTLE rolls his eyes to heaven in sardonic martyrdom and returns to work on HALSY's bike while HALSY on the other hand grunts and grumbles comfortably gnawing a stale doughnut he didn't pay for.

> HALSY
>
> And if their machine blows up they don't have to put out one nickel on it, factory-sponsored bastards!

Pasture

Gray ovals of grazing sheep spot a vast rolling pasture washed in the leaning light of evening.

Then one by one these critters lift their heads and listen, at first still masticating but then struck still in a mounting motionlessness that will soon be flight.

We hear faintly the engines and the Indian yells of motorized cowboys and then into view over the crest of the hill come HALSY and LITTLE, scooter-mounted and roaring drunk.

They dive through the sheep, dividing the herd repeatedly as again and again the terrified animals re-form into a loping mass that spills down the hillside; they circle and spin through the billowing grass and whoop it up in an imitation roundup that becomes by degrees less out of hand and more expert at controlling this bahing woolly tide. Until gunshots from the distance bring them to a halt and then they streak out of sight over the hill whence they came, followed by an outraged, jeep-mounted shepherd.

Fauss Kitchen

MOM and SEALLY sit at an oilcloth-covered table in a ramshackle but completely outfitted kitchen. They are idly playing with the remains of a meal; one place, still neatly set, yawns pointedly. They have gone ahead and eaten without LITTLE for perhaps the first time in their lives, and it has made a meal composed of hurt fury and fear. Now a call from an enraged sheep rancher in the vicinity has confounded their emotions further.

MOM

We want to hear Little's side before we start leaping at conclusions, Seal.

SEALLY

What did you say dessert was?

MOM

I got Whip and Wonder, Wet and Warm or Slit and Serve tonight.

SEALLY

Don't matter to me.

MOM

Whichever. Speak up.

SEALLY

Won't stay with me twenty minutes.

She gets up with their plates.

MOM

Because it just don't sound like Little to me, hounding sheep on a sackle.

SEALLY

Where is he, then?

MOM

It's not humanitary.

SEALLY

Old Frazier seen him.

MOM

Someone with a sackle. That don't mean Little. Specially being two of them. We're the only buddies Little wants, you know that. He don't have no friends.

SEALLY

Then he's lying dead somewhere and we're eating dessert.

The door to the back porch opens and a smashed LITTLE sticks his head in.

LITTLE

Hi.

SEALLY

(*After a moment*) I'll have my Whip and Wonder, Mom.

MOM

Where'd you come from? I never heard your bike.

Wearing a fixed and silly smile, LITTLE opens the door wider to admit HALSY.

LITTLE

This here's my friend I brought home.

HALSY nods. Around his neck he wears his ill-gotten camera.

LITTLE

Remember Sideburns? This here's Sideburns from last night.

SEALLY

Dinner's done.

LITTLE

Oh, we ate.

HALSY

No thank you, sir. We ate.

SEALLY

Hawdy Frazier called to say some bums on bikes were tearing up his Riverroad acres until he run 'em off.

LITTLE

Well, we already ate so we'll just hit the sack.

And he moves toward the hall almost on tiptoe, as though there were people sleeping of whom he must be considerate.

SEALLY

Hold on, Little.

MOM

Your father's speaking to you.

LITTLE

I don't feel good.

MOM

I don't wonder.

Rubbing LITTLE's back, energetically HALSY pushes him toward the hall and escape.

HALSY

You got to go to work in the morning, Little. I think you ought to get to bed.

SEALLY

Okay, Sideburns, I told you two hold on.

MOM

Seally, peace.

LITTLE

I told Sideburns he could stay all night.

HALSY

Just until the weekend.

LITTLE

He's waiting on a part coming from Farmington, so I told him he could stay on here.

Silence.

LITTLE

(*Funny, fake anger*) Hey listen, what time is it? I got to get up in the morning.

And he ducks out into the dark hall, leaving HALSY with his parents.

HALSY

I got to look for a job too in the morning. Can't draw my unemployment out here until May. So you don't know any positions open, do you? I did have this job in Texas but my old lady wouldn't go out there and leave all her girlfriends.

Feeling secure and at home, he puts the camera on the table and sits down.

HALSY

Screw her, right? I mean, I had this job right up until Christmas and she wouldn't come out there. Hell, I don't care. I can get a job any time I want to over at Mira Linda.

SEALLY

Then, Sideburns, I suggest you go to Mira Linda.

MOM

Would you want a cup of coffee first?

But HALSY rejects both suggestions and heads for the hall.

HALSY

Where'd that Little get to? I got to take a piss.

And he exits after LITTLE.

45

MOM

(*After a moment*) You want Instant Fross on this, or just plain?

SEALLY

Don't matter beans to me. It'll go right through me tonight.

Little's Bedroom

Removing shoes and socks, jackets, shirts and pants, LITTLE and HALSY tiptoe around the room as though silence would redeem them.

LITTLE gets an idea. He calls for attention with broad drunken gestures. He takes an LP from the shelf and puts it on the phonograph and then before the sound begins he reveals the album face to HALSY, counting on the latter's bliss.

Sounds of the Grand Prix.

HALSY grabs the album hungrily and settles on the bed in dirty shorts and t-shirt. LITTLE lies on the floor. They face each other enraptured and pick their toes and listen, as though it were Tchaikovsky, to the deafening sound of over a hundred motorcycles.

Elder Fauss's Bedroom

MOM is in bed in the shadowy dark; she wears a headset connected to a portable radio on the nightstand.

The sound of the Grand Prix continues, slightly less deafening here.

46

The bathroom door is partly open and a wedge of light falls across the floor; through the Grand Prix noise we hear SEALLY's plaintive painful groaning from within.

Little's Bedroom

In their euphoria, HALSY and LITTLE have slumped into repose and finally sleep as the Grand TT at Sachsen-Ring continues, with German commentary.

Desert Enduro

A *wide-angle view* of what seems an unending row of motorcycles revving up at the start of this race recalls that picture of the opening up of the Oklahoma Territory where a lineup of buggies and schooners were gathered together for an all-at-once dash into the wilderness. Today's occasion is a sporting event, however, consisting largely of amateurs, with no such stakes and only minor weekend glory.

Moving at a *closer angle* down this line, we see mostly men and pimpled youth all one extreme or the other, cadaverous or plump—one man so heavy he can navigate only with the aid of crutches and must be helped onto his bike by friends; once there, though, he will stay aloft thanks mainly to balance and momentum.

And among these men are tough women, masked and mounted determinedly, with swelling buttocks and thighs; and weird, unworldly children stretched between pedal and handlebar like eerie monkeys.

In campers and trailers and pickups and trucks, de-
pendents and relatives hold their ears and squint into
the dust. We are far out in the desert and the Sunday
noon has begun to pound.

We join LITTLE and HALSY at the starting line, the former
helmeted and poised and ready to go, though it seems
too soon; the latter carrying his helmet and leaning
leisurely against his bike as he zips up his leathers from
a more than pointed depth. He wears an Australian
jolly jumbuck hat and if by a glance he communicates
with a GIRL on the sidelines (MONETH, GIRL 2) it would
not be uncharacteristic of him in these mounting seconds
before the race begins; it would be in fact his reckless
brand of gamesmanship.

LITTLE at the same time is muttering some prayerful
formula for winning, a mannerism we will become accustomed to in later races. He interrupts these devotions
only to pass a concerned, anxious look to HALSY, if such
can be communicated through glasses, helmet and visor,
and HALSY gestures a request to the flagman to wait,
a formal signal recognized in professional racing, but
seeming a little grand and postured here.

HALSY mounts his bike. He tosses his jumbuck hat to
GIRL 2 on the sidelines and as he puts first a hairnet
and then his helmet on, he dares to take his time even
further and, grinning, leans down and shouts under
LITTLE's shield his estimate of GIRL 2, comments which
are heard by no one, considering the din, but which
cause GIRL 2 to blush nonetheless.

Now ready, he gives a thumbs-up gesture of encouragement to the crouched and eager LITTLE, whose lips in-

voluntarily recite the mumbo-jumbo of his concentration; then he wags his thumb lasciviously at GIRL 2, who is round and featureless, plaintive and available and all but a duplicate of her predecessor in HALSY's life.

The race begins and, true to his swagger, HALSY is off at once on his rear wheel, riding aloft until swallowed in smoke and dust.

Pelted by grit, GIRL 2 squints after her hero devotedly.

As the name implies, enduros tend to be long races, in this case some five hours over a variety of rugged terrain, hills, jagged rocks and sand pits. It is hot and dusty and full of spills since many riders are without experience and those who have competed before tend to be rather aggressive. Also, there are different classifications racing together and so the action can and does get, in the vernacular, hairy.

Once sufficient excitement of a general nature has been established, we concentrate on the contrasting racing styles of LITTLE and HALSY, the one narrow, oblivious and unswerving, concentrated and plodding; the other, rash, showy and unpredictable.

Separately at this point neither HALSY nor LITTLE would qualify as an intelligent racer, and what is worse it seems in connection their peculiar characteristics spell trouble.

HALSY is playful. He paces himself to LITTLE and then pulls ahead as though to stimulate a more specific contest between himself and his friend. In view of the long pull, however, this takes energies LITTLE doesn't care to expend and so he resists the challenge. With the result that HALSY moves in closer. The game ends badly. Their bikes tangle and they both go down in a shower of sand and sparks.

The accident seems serious. The two men remain inert for several moments, some distance apart. It is LITTLE who recovers first. Using what strength he has, and limping badly, he gets his bike off the track as other racers continue past.

LITTLE

Hals? Halsy?

Dragging a lifeless leg and fearing the worst, LITTLE makes his way to his unmoving friend—to find HALSY still lives, flat on his back and motionless but raging heavenward.

LITTLE

You okay?

HALSY

You ran right under me, you birdbrained fart!

LITTLE

I think my leg's broke.

HALSY sits up.

HALSY

What the hell did you run right under me for?

LITTLE

You hurt any?

HALSY

I blew my thrash, I think.

50

LITTLE

Yeah, your thrash is busted.

HALSY

Jeese, you're a screwup, Little!

LITTLE

Yeah, I broke my leg too, I think.

HALSY

How's your bike?

LITTLE

May 'a got dirt in it, I don't know. But I broke my leg.

HALSY

You got a duck wrench?

LITTLE

What are you going to do?

HALSY checks the broken thrash on his bike to see if it is not too hot to remove.

HALSY

What choice do I got?

LITTLE

Take my bike, why don't you.

HALSY

Then I'm disqualified for sure, brainless wonder. Changing bikes.

LITTLE

(*Painfully disappointed*) I thought you was going for help.

HALSY

Even we changed numbers and leathers, some joker'd spot me and start whining rules.

LITTLE

I couldn't even get out of my leathers, Hals, my leg's broke.

HALSY

Okay, your leg's broken, I heard you. Shut up.

HALSY marches anxiously to LITTLE's bike. He removes the desired wrench from a tool pack and works at getting the hot thrash off, scowling and cursing at every bike that passes grinding out grit.

LITTLE watches, hurting and forlorn.

HALSY returns to his own bike to replace his broken thrash with LITTLE's.

HALSY
(*As he works*) You got matches?

LITTLE

Matches?

HALSY

Yeah hell, if I don't get back before dark, you don't want to freeze.

LITTLE

(*Alarm.*) They'll get somebody out here for me before dark.

HALSY

Not these Mickey Mouse country shows, man. They don't take responsibility for no one. You're on your own.

LITTLE

(*Panic.*) Well heck, Halsy, you'll be back for me before dark. It's only four o'clock.

HALSY

Sure I'll be back. I just meant in case.

LITTLE

In case what? You coming back or not? I got a broke leg.

HALSY

Don't panic, man. You panic in this weather, it'll kill you.

LITTLE

Yeah, and there's probably snakes around here too, damnit.

Ready to go, HALSY reaches into his pack and throws a small kit to LITTLE.

LITTLE

What's this?

HALSY

It's what to do in case of snake bite. Read it.

He mounts his bike.

HALSY

You want to learn to take care of yourself, Little. Just watch me.

And blowing a kiss to LITTLE, he rejoins the race. The sound of his motor quickly dies in the distance. By now the stragglers have all passed and LITTLE is assailed by silence bulging with heat and the occasional ominous crunch of gravel, suggesting scorpions and sidewinders.

Enduro Finish

The sun is beyond the mountains and shadows stretch across the desert. A short column of winners still astride their bikes wait through a poorly planned trophy ceremony attended mainly by kids.

HALSY has won for his class. He takes a deep swallow of beer and then kisses GIRL 2, whom he accommodates sidesaddle on his cycle. His hand travels up the front of her t-shirt and cups over one breast.

> HALSY
>
> Say, you ought to be a model.

> GIRL 2
>
> Quit it.

> HALSY
>
> No, I mean it.

GIRL 2 squirms to free herself, embarrassed at such open play, but HALSY persists, concealing his pleasure behind an air of objective appreciation.

> HALSY
>
> Listen no, I'm an expert. You know how many races I won?

> GIRL 2
>
> Do you have to do that?

> HALSY
>
> And every time, out comes some trophy girl thinks she's Ann-Margret.

> GIRL 2
>
> I never said I was any Ann-Margret.

HALSY

These hands have held the boobs of more top-flight actresses and model trophy girls—

GIRL 2

I'm not any trophy girl. Now come on!

HALSY

And you got every one of them beat, my dear, by a mile. (*Belches seductively.*) At least a mile. Two miles.

GIRL 2

(*Tightly*) They don't have no trophy girls in desert enduros, you know that.

HALSY

Yeah, cheap bastards. All this racing and no pussy.

GIRL 2

Please take your hands off my things.

HALSY obliges with mock emotion.

HALSY

Boy, people sure don't know how to take a compliment.

GIRL 2

(*Reached*) I thank you but, my gosh, in public?

He whispers a blunt suggestion in her ear. She shakes her head in a flexible no.

HALSY

Why not?

GIRL 2

Well, for one thing you haven't even got your trophy yet.

HALSY pushes his pedal down and starts his engine.

HALSY
Damn if I don't!

And as the official approaches with clipboard and puny statuette, HALSY bursts from the line of winners and zooms away, GIRL 2 unwilling but holding on for dear life.

The other winners, clutching their gilt and fragile trophies to their laps, watch HALSY disappear down the road into the romantic shadows of evening with GIRL 2, and suppose forlornly that his reward is greater than their own.

Desert Night

LITTLE shivers beside a small twig fire. His head rests on the saddle of his bike. Frightened, he listens for noises in the night. Naturally a coyote wails—none too distantly.

LITTLE
(*Loudly*) When do the other guys get back, Joe and Bill? (*Other voice*) Oh, they should be back any minute, Don. More coffee, Larry? How about you, Spike? (*Other voice*) Thanks, Joe. (*Other voice*) You're welcome, George, I mean Bill.

Now he sees the distant lights of a vehicle coming through the desert night, rising and falling with the terrain and sometimes dropping out of sight altogether.

Anxious to be found, he throws a few more twigs on the fire to brighten it, those he was saving for the long night. Every movement is painful.

Pickup Interior

The pickup bounces along over a rough road, LITTLE
wincing with every jolt. HALSY is behind the wheel, and
between them is GIRL 2, hooked and hollowed.

> HALSY
>
> Sometimes I really have to give myself credit.
> I should have been a genius or something.

> LITTLE
>
> I don't know, though. It's dishonest.

> HALSY
>
> What can they do if they catch you?

> LITTLE
>
> What?

> HALSY
>
> Only suspend you.

> LITTLE
>
> Maybe it's not really broken.

> HALSY
>
> And you're no worse off suspended when you
> can't ride anyway with a broke leg. And hell
> I'm suspended already, so they can't touch me.

> LITTLE
>
> (*In pain*) Try going a little slower, could you?

> HALSY
>
> Okay, now then listen. It's really great—

> LITTLE
>
> No, I mean drive a little slower or I'm going to . . .

How's your leg?

Oh, it's . . .

He faints against the window with a thud.

Receiving Room

It is late at night in a small country hospital. A NURSE and a DOCTOR are working on an only partly conscious LITTLE. Dark corridors and shadows surround, enclosing HALSY and GIRL 2.

HALSY

(*Continuing*) They got pro races every weekend in California some place and if we split out there who's going to know who's you and who's me?

LITTLE

Somebody could.

HALSY

Boy, you think you're famous.

LITTLE

Listen to you talk you took money at every TT and half-miler in the whole United States.

HALSY

Funny thing, nobody knows me in California. So how they going to tell I'm not you if I got your license and your bike and your number and you're right there to deny it.

LITTLE

How are you intending we split?

HALSY

Halves. And all the points go automatic under your name, not mine, toward your expert card and your standing in the Nationals. Which the way you ride is the only way you'll ever qualify. Is someone race for you. And you act like you doing me a favor, shit.

Fauss Kitchen

Later that night. MOM and SEALLY, in their bathrobes, sit stunned and robbed at the kitchen table while LITTLE, on crutches and further burdened by his suit case, is failing to make his exit smooth and unemotional.

LITTLE

Seems like a pretty good deal, the way I look at it.

SEALLY

Who for?

MOM

Oh yeah, a very good deal!

SEALLY

For Sideburns!

LITTLE

If I want to race pro, where can I race pro around here?

MOM

Well, Dad, sell your stalls. We're out of racing.

SEALLY

You're his tuner, Little, what are you talking about racing? On your bike with your license because he's been throwed out.

LITTLE

Meantime I can hit some big events, Dad, in California. Which I can't do around here.

SEALLY

Sideburns is racing, dummy, not you.

MOM

And meantime who pays?

SEALLY

And I think he's done it on purpose.

LITTLE

Broke my leg?

MOM

What's a broke leg to his kind?

LITTLE

You'll have to prove that to me.

SEALLY regards the camera hanging on the hall door.

SEALLY

Maybe I'll do just that.

Outside in the night HALSY honks the horn of his pickup. Silence follows in the kitchen.

LITTLE

(*Finally*) Well, I got to go now.

SEALLY

Best of fortune to you, Little. Though I don't see

no good coming out of teaming up with undesirables.

He shakes LITTLE's hand and MOM leans up to brush
LITTLE's cheek with hers.

> MOM
> That goes ditto for me.

The car honks again.

> LITTLE
> I know what you all mean, but there's a lot I
> can learn if I'm going to race and some I can
> show him too.

Again the horn.

> SEALLY
> He's going to have the neighbors down on us.

> LITTLE
> (*Wanting their blessing*) And what else is there
> to do?

But no blessing is forthcoming.

> LITTLE
> Besides, we're going to split fifty-fifty, so how
> can I lose?

Pickup Exterior

LITTLE lies in the rear of the pickup with his bike. It is the
middle of the night and it is raining and he is cold
and wet and wind-buffeted as the car speeds down
the highway.

He crawls up and pounds on the window of the cab.

Pickup Interior

HALSY drives through the night. His eyes are tired. GIRL 2 is asleep on the seat beside him, her feet up and her head in his lap. He turns when LITTLE pounds on the window.

> LITTLE
> (*Shouting from outside*) It's raining!

HALSY puts his finger to his lips to indicate sh-sh-sh somebody's sleeping.

Pickup Exterior

> LITTLE
> (*Furious*) I'm not supposed to get my cast wet!

Pickup Interior

Now LITTLE is at the wheel, managing to drive despite his heavy foot. As it was loneliness as much as bad weather that prompted his complaints from the rear of the truck he now stares ahead through the rain-streaked windshield disgruntled and forlorn, since, though inside, he is still alone.

Pickup Exterior

Rain falls on the covered bike and onto a zipped-up sleeping bag palpitating with HALSY and GIRL 2 screwing.

California Night Flat Track

Practice laps are in progress and single cycles sprint around the track. A long line of bikes divides the pits as racers wait their turns, accompanied by their crews. The object being to get as many turns as possible before the race proper, riders coming off the track after the allotted practice time get in line again immediately, re-tuning their engines as gradually they move their bikes toward start-finish.

LITTLE, his leg still in a cast, holds his bike and hops forward as space allows, watching the trials intently and betweentimes checking out his engine with the agitated guesswork of mechanical genius; his rider, however, is not in evidence.

Instead, elsewhere in the pits, HALSY in a three-cornered black-felt pilgrim's hat stands by a latter-day BLACK-SMITH with portable blowtorch who adjusts the measurements of his steel skidshoe. HALSY's leathers, as usual, are flamboyantly unzipped and reveal his personality.

The BLACKSMITH presents the shoe to HALSY, who squats down and tries it on. The shoe needs additional adjustment and HALSY returns it to the BLACKSMITH.

HALSY

(*Shouting over the noise*) Make it right, baby.

He thumbs his chest importantly.

HALSY

(*Shouting*) Número uno!

BLACKSMITH

(*Indifferent*) Sí sí, señor.

LITTLE moves closer to the starting line and feeling anxious and abused, he looks around for HALSY.

As we study the nature of the average dirt track:

An official at the head of the line of bikes checks the rider's number against his clipboard as each pushes his cycle past this point.

The next official at the track edge halts the rider until some of those already practicing are signaled in by the flagman to make room for those waiting.

There is some serious sprinting in these practice laps and as well some disheartening failures of man and machine.

Touring the grandstands we observe bundled-up wives and children;

And yellow-haired, balloon-coiffed teenage girls clustered excitedly at the fence. At any lull in the engine roar these girls yell across the track to the pits to some lank hero a paean more taunting than awed;

At the snack shack, GIRL 2 smears mustard on a hotdog;

Hawkers sell motorcycle magazines; a few cops haunt the scene; youths swagger by;

Kids climb over the fences and scale signboards for views of spectacular vantage.

In the pits again, a scrawny young man on his hands and knees, wearing only his underwear, affixes a squared, boxy 95 with masking tape to the back of his leathers, which are spread flat as a paper doll on the greasy dust.

Another man, breathless and roly-poly, pushes his bike at a run; it will not start; he all but disappears into the distance still on foot.

And all kinds of mechanics work on all kinds of bikes. It would be impossible to exaggerate the features and feathers and moods found here in the pits among tuners and kin. Germanic shaved heads and waxed mustaches predominate, but there is also the long, curly hair of the times, framing faces of shriveled gloom. Conjunctivitis is prevalent: enormous guts and running sores. Some of these men have no ears, and some have fewer fingers than normal. Many, like LITTLE, seem almost sightless behind thick glasses thumbprinted with grease. And all are stuffed into white workpants so tight a smudged relief of comb and wallet is stamped on every rear, while a small wad in front could be either penis or car keys.

LITTLE waits and moves toward start-finish. Impatient for HALSY, he nonetheless concentrates on the riders circling the track, a fixed attention that is broken only to examine his thumb and forefinger now and then when his constant nervous digging at his neck and shoulders yields some treasured nougat of congealed waste.

HALSY shows up only when LITTLE is almost to start-finish. He transfers his three-cornered hat from his head to LITTLE's, puts on his hairnet and then his helmet. He mounts the bike as LITTLE stands by, tickling the engine.

The official motions HALSY forward, then gestures him onto the track.

LITTLE gains higher ground in order to watch HALSY's practice laps. Perched on a log on his one good foot, he turns with HALSY's movement around the track. As HALSY approaches start-finish again, LITTLE extends his arm to set his stopwatch.

Once again he follows HALSY around the track, listening with all his might, his clock-watch arm outstretched and his attention so acute and squinted it resembles pain. But in this slow turn he loses his balance and his heavy cast pulls him from the log before HALSY gets the flag.

HALSY continues around the track before he coasts into the rear of the pits and again gets in line.

LITTLE hobbles up and takes over the support of the bike as HALSY removes his helmet and unzips his leathers. Adrenaline charges their speech and actions.

HALSY
Damn, I can do better than that. What did I do?

LITTLE, adept with his cast, squats down to check out the bike.

LITTLE
I want to tight up your boil packets.

HALSY
Damn dirt's so damn loose and oily they ought to tear it all up and start fresh.

LITTLE
You know where they get that dirt, don't you?

HALSY
What'd I do, man? Where's the watch?

Buy it from the cemetery.

HALSY pulls the stopwatch from LITTLE's pocket.

HALSY

What was it?

LITTLE

I fell down.

HALSY

Little, you ain't good for nothing.

LITTLE

You get a tuner good as me. You got the best damn scooter here.

HALSY crouches and angrily adjusts his skidshoe.

HALSY

Damn skidshoe ain't right yet.

LITTLE

You going to be hotshoeing it around cemetery dirt, Halsy, you better be saying your prayers and not be cussing everybody out.

HALSY

I'm not the one falls down every time I stand up, buddy. I don't have to say my prayers. You're the one falls down every time you stand up.

LITTLE

Cemetery dirt right out of the cemetery.

HALSY

Can't even time one lap without falling down, and you're not even on a bike.

LITTLE

You didn't know that, did you . . . cemetery sur-
plus dirt.

HALSY studies the track while LITTLE cleans the tires
on the bike.

HALSY

I ain't afraid of any damn spooks.

LITTLE

All tracks, that's where they get their dirt.

HALSY

What I am afraid of is, you get a bad track
like this and it slows down us glory boys till
we're swimming with all them no-nothing guys
and you can get in messes there around them
turns all crowded up.

LITTLE straightens up.

LITTLE

That's one thing you didn't even know, I bet.

HALSY

What?

LITTLE

That that's where all that dirt comes from.

HALSY

The cemetery. I knew that.

LITTLE

Don't sound like it to me, cussing and blasfaming
up and down a streak.

(*Wistfully*) I just pray to stay erect, that's all I ask.

If I was you, I'd just say my prayers to stay erect.

The line of bikes moves slowly toward the track.

Start-Finish

This is the final race of the night. About fifteen cycles are in place, among them HALSY's, just arriving, and a few others as well, moving in.

(*Loudspeaker*) Number 47, Hanson Dowel, Bultaco-mounted. Number 82, Denny Pitman, Honda-mounted. Number 102, Tobel Schwab . . .

After one name there may be no response or applause. After another, a surge of hooray and excitement is heard when a rider's whole family and graduating class seem to be present. In some cases the rider is that well known and such acknowledgment is justified. In other cases the very obscurity of the man demands some show of enthusiasm, if only comic.

The ANNOUNCER continues as HALSY fusses with his skid-shoe and LITTLE, in the pits, stares transfixed, drained and expectant and blanched and eerie in the kliegs.

(*Loudspeaker*) . . . on a Harley-Davidson, Zenith distributors, 1768 North Zenith, who wants you to know, yes, they are open Sundays and invites you all to drop in after the church of your choice. Number 11X, Gentry Bowls on his famed Suzuki, and beside him, new to California racing, Number 65, Little Fauss, Contralto-mounted . . .

In the stands, GIRL 2 gives a vigorous cheer. But it goes sour before it concludes, for at the same time another GIRL (3), not much different in appearance, has done likewise, cheered old HALSY. Each deceived into believing herself his only fan, the two GIRLS now regard each other stunned and disappointed, a shock converting to hostile hurt as each sits down again to sulk and glare.

At start-finish HALSY shrugs and acknowledges each woman with the gesture of an upright thumb and a self-satisfied smile of happy guilt. More important at the moment is the race, and HALSY takes it seriously. Friday night dirt tracks are professional races with hard competition and no place for clowns. Helmeted and poised, the braggart disappears into the professional.

Now they are all primed and roaring and chomping with puffs of blue exhaust.

The flagman on the platform whips the air with his pennant.

Riders accelerate.

Their positions change into melee.

Spectators and pitmen lean forward to discern some degree of early standing, since nothing the barking ANNOUNCER now says is intelligible.

LITTLE hops wildly to his vantage on the log, his heavy leg swinging. When he finally finds HALSY on the back stretch, his expression is hopeful, though HALSY is seventh or eighth at least. LITTLE's good foot twists slowly on the log as his body turns with the progress of the race.

The two GIRLS in the stands are more aware of each other than of their hero, and as HALSY passes below them their cheers are more combatant than unanimous.

We stay with this contest, which is ten laps, and watch HALSY's gradual advance toward the lead. That he win would be unrealistic in view of the competition, but it is vital to be in the money, so second or third place is fought for as fiercely as first.

Due as much to the misfortune of others as to his own reckless skill, HALSY's position in the race improves steadily.

And LITTLE, aloft on the log in the middle of the track, is serious and shadowed, if not actually prayerful.

The crowd stands as the top five or six racers barrel down the front straight, HALSY among them.

"Come on, Halsy!" "Come on, Halsy!" Alas, each GIRL must now recognize in the other the privileged information which was her own claim to superior intimacy: HALSY is HALSY and not LITTLE, O perfidy, and see herself as more sorely rivaled than before.

A spill. The ambulance crawls forward, its red light radiating the misery and fatality that alone removes the round and round from routine.

LITTLE, in a wild, accelerated limp, dashes among others across the backfield of the pits. The others outdistance him. He stops. Officials wave the remaining riders around the pileup, among them HALSY, still in the race and now third.

With the same enormous, urgent limp, LITTLE hurries back to start-finish as the racers pass the yellow flag on the last lap, HALSY moving up past the second racer with a push that is no less exciting for being cliché.

Now we take the last lap with HALSY as he moves heroically if hopelessly against the racer in the lead. Putt-putt puny and arrogant, they fight it out.

In the pits, LITTLE leaps around on one foot, addressing the air with enthusiasm and demanding acknowledgment and praise from nonexistent friends and associates.

HALSY doesn't win, but he comes close, and in this league that's good. He glides into the pits with the straight-back grace of the champ transformed by performance from the goof into the god, and whooping and screaming, LITTLE hobbles toward him.

Enough cannot be said of LITTLE's leaping. Inhibited by the dual constraints of his cast and the aborted impulses of physical contact, his excitement finds no outlet but jumping into the air around HALSY, who is equally at a loss and merely shakes his head in uncharacteristic disbelief as he removes the eggshell of his helmet and divides the hot placenta of his leathers to find himself born a hero. Perhaps placing second is the initial legitimate accomplishment of his life so far, and he is stunned into modesty.

HALSY

This damn bike, man, used them other scooters for traction!

LITTLE

One more lap, one more even quarter mile, and you'd 'a been first!

HALSY

You know what even second pays? Screw first!

LITTLE

Beer's on you, man, for a week!

HALSY

Beer nothing. I'm getting me a pint!

They have waltzed around in the need to consummate this joy, but as they are not really friends there is no embrace, only the sense of its absence.

Grandstand Gate

GIRLS 2 and 3 are amid the pileup of friends, fans and relatives waiting to get across the track to the pits now that the race is over. They examine each other coolly, and when the gate is open and the crowd chokes through, they angrily jostle each other for first position.

Pits

LITTLE and HALSY are as they were, though the pits are filling up now with spectators, and HALSY, ever uncomfortable without a costume, has recovered his three-cornered hat.

LITTLE pays a vendor for two paper cups of beer.

HALSY

(*Adrenaline flowing.*) He fell right in my groove,
man. Hell, I took two laps before they even got
him out of there. You see that. Is he dead or
anything?

LITTLE, who was at this point raising his cup in untimely
toast, darkens as the two GIRLS arrive to flank HALSY.

GIRL 3

I just want to ask you one thing, Halsy Knox,
and that's, who the hell is she?

GIRL 2

Who the hell am I? Who the hell are you, you
mean.

Unresponding to their rage, HALSY brings them both into
a bear hug, one arm around the neck of each, and
continues excitedly to LITTLE, who has, alas, been turned
off by this intrusion.

HALSY

(*Still exhilarated*) Man, it's just so darn much
fun. Even though I'm working so hard just sitting
up there. In that position it's just so darn exciting.

LITTLE crouches soberly down to the bike and sits on
his cast.

LITTLE

It still surges. Down the chute. I could hear that
much.

Holding his beer to the lips of the GIRL on his left,
HALSY kisses the GIRL on his right; he then transfers
the beer to his right hand and while he kisses the GIRL

on his left he refreshes the GIRL on his right; his arms
remain around their necks throughout and their resistance
is slight, though their dignity requires that they snarl
occasionally.

> HALSY
> (*Continuing as above*) I know if I can just get
> in position I can sit in there all night. Except
> you got to work so hard you can't enjoy it.

Pickup Interior

A flashlight glares in our eyes, then darts light and
reflection unsteadily as HALSY climbs into the cab of
the pickup, a little drunkenly and half dressed but in
his costume hat.

> HALSY
> (*An attempt at whispering that comes and goes.*)
> What are you sleeping in the car for?

LITTLE is torn between sleep and embarrassment.

> LITTLE
> Somebody's got to guard the bike.

> HALSY
> I'll guard the bike. Go on in if you want to.

> LITTLE
> (*Stalling*) Where'd you get the flashlight?

> HALSY
> Hey, look at this flashlight, man. It cleans up

lint, air-conditions your face, and it's got a table on the side tells weights and measures.

He puts it in the glove compartment.

> LITTLE
>
> You just going to cop it off her?

> HALSY
>
> (*His justification*) You know you can get a ticket if those safety patrols stop you on the highway and you ain't got the proper emergency safety equipment? (*Beat.*) You going in?

> LITTLE
>
> I guess I won't bother.

> HALSY
>
> It's okay by me. Just tell 'em I said it was okay.

> LITTLE
>
> I think I'm . . . (*Cough cough.*) . . . coming down with a cold or something.

> HALSY
>
> Okay then, let's split.

> LITTLE
>
> You mean cut out on Moneth?

> HALSY
>
> Yeah. Hold on a second, I'll be right back.

Driveway

HALSY leaves the pickup stealthily and in bare feet hurries to the back door of a dingy bungalow.

Bungalow Interior

He lets himself in the back door of the darkened house, silent except for the purple strings of some low-keyed music to screw by on the phonograph.

He collects his shoes and shirt from the disheveled living room. A tray is on the coffee table with a bottle of booze and other dismal refreshment. He adds his shoes to the tray and prepares to take the whole thing as the record player clicks startlingly and the record begins again.

Holding the tray and tiptoeing, he moves through the sleeping house once again to the back door just opening.

LITTLE appears.

Driveway

Shirt over his bare shoulders, shoes and booze on the tray, HALSY elbows LITTLE back outside.

> HALSY
> (*Heavy, impatient whisper*) What do you want?

> LITTLE
> (*Having reconsidered*) Well, my cold's not *too* bad . . .

> HALSY
> Man, we're leaving.

> LITTLE
> Shouldn't I say goodbye to Moneth?

> HALSY
> To hell with her. What's Moneth to you?

Well, nothing. But if, like you say, it's such a
setup in there . . .

Anxious to leave, HALSY edges toward the pickup.

HALSY

Forget it.

LITTLE

But now's probably a good time to take care
of this shyness I got and, you know, kind of
strike while the iron's hot. Long as no one cares.

HALSY

You had your chance. Now come on.

LITTLE

Couldn't I just look?

Bedroom

In the soft glow of a frilly bed lamp, GIRLS 2 and 3
present a nude landscape on the bed to HALSY and LITTLE
standing at the door of this small bedroom, HALSY still
carrying the tray.

LITTLE

(*Plaintive whisper*) They're going to feel real bad
when they wake up and you're gone.

HALSY

(*Righteous whisper*) No sir, man, once a chick
swings AC-DC on you, split.

A *closeup* of HALSY reveals his bitter guilt.

Once it's cool, but twice it's queer.

And he gestures a reluctant, touched and hungry LITTLE to move on.

Pickup Interior

HALSY is slumped down against the passenger door and is drunker than before, as LITTLE, his cast a discomfort but no handicap, drives the pickup through the night.

HALSY

Little?

LITTLE

What?

HALSY

Are you awake?

LITTLE

I better be. I'm driving.

HALSY

Oh, yeah, you're driving.

LITTLE

You're drunk.

HALSY

If I tell you something. You got to believe me, okay?

LITTLE

I believe whatever anybody tells me.

HALSY

Not this, you won't.

LITTLE

I don't know what the truth is if it's not what
people say.

HALSY

You see me make out good all the time, don't you?
Well, I don't make out good at all. (*Beat.*) Those
girls, you know? You think I don't know they're
dogs?

LITTLE

I didn't know if you knew or not.

HALSY

I don't know why with all I got going for me
all I ever get is the real pigs.

LITTLE

Well, they mean well, I guess.

HALSY

You think I don't know what they are?

LITTLE

I didn't know if they were or not.

HALSY

Sometimes drunk it seems like they're just prin-
cesses. But always I wake up in the morning and
it's a pig.

LITTLE

I just figured you like pigs.

HALSY

Moneth was pretty bad, huh?

LITTLE

I just figured you wanted a pretty girl or someone decent, all you'd do is snap your finger.

HALSY

That's what I'm telling you, man! It's just these gland cases and hurting whores who'll have me. And queers.

LITTLE

Boy, are you drunk.

To recover from the open show of hurt and wonder, HALSY tries to pull himself up a little.

HALSY

Yeah, where the hell are we?

They drive in silence for a while, HALSY staring out the window at his own reflection against the night.

HALSY

(*Finally*) Stay clean, man.

LITTLE

Oh, I'm not so clean.

HALSY

I don't mean pure.

LITTLE

Sometimes you ought to see my thoughts.

HALSY

I mean decent.

LITTLE

Hell, I'm not your just pure St. Peter, Halsy, just because I don't talk it up all the time.

HALSY slumps down again and closes his eyes as though to go to sleep. It is silent again for a while.

HALSY

You know what?

LITTLE

What?

HALSY

All I say is just talk.

He has not opened his eyes. He might be concealing feeling or he might be halfway to sleep.

LITTLE

Yeah, well you must talk good because you had two girls in the sack while dumb I was out sleeping in the car.

HALSY

I wish I'd been there . . .

In a moment the remark seems odd to LITTLE. He looks over, but HALSY is obviously asleep and the words have come from his unconscious.

LITTLE turns back to the road, his eyes tired, his mood disconcerted. A slow *crossfade* begins, and the figure of the naked girl that takes shape before his eyes can seem for a while to be a product of his imagination.

Golden Slopes

It is a bright sunny day and down this barren, burnished incline a naked girl stumbles. She is alone in the landscape and at some distance. She would seem by her walk, if nothing else, to be drunk, for she staggers and slumps through the weeds. Yet it is with a peculiar pride and determination that she approaches. Her name is RITA NEBRASKA and she holds her head high.

Another Angle

Places these slopes above a country raceway and

Other Angles

Take us to the public address stand, where the announcer and several officials are on their feet and lean out, stunned and unbelieving, at the sight of RITA's descent.

Scanning with binoculars, one official picks out a cluster of UNDESIRABLES encamped like Indians at the hillside, and with the advantage of this *telephoto view* we see the familiar greasy grins of this dedicatedly asocial group and understand RITA's nakedness then to be the depraved extension of their noted playful savagery.

A second and closer look at RITA as she continues her journey toward the track fails to say more of what prompts this bare-assed pilgrimage through rocks and brambles. Stoned by fear, shame, determination, or mindless on drugs, it is all the same. She is rigid and expressionless, and only a dim negative courage holds her together.

The official leaves the public-address booth and crosses down to the track. Riders are in place to begin a race now delayed, among them HALSY.

The flagman, angered by the interruption, looks in the direction indicated by the official.

Again on RITA, we can only guess what motivates this weird approach. Is she acting out a dare imposed on her by the UNDESIRABLES? Is she fleeing them? Or, rather, is she their emissary, carrying some ultimatum?

At the track, the start is called off and LITTLE and HALSY stare up the slope in disbelief.

To the UNDESIRABLES, who dominate the hilltop and cluster nervously about their bikes as though ready to attack or flee.

Spectators who line the fence begin now one by one to notice RITA. They squint at first and then respond uncomfortably. Some stare morbidly as at an accident. Others turn away and gather up their families into reassuring bundles. A few leer and laugh for a moment, but then fall silent as some chilling nightmare of their own comes back.

As RITA gets closer, we see her eyes are rimmed with charcoal and dilated. They do not focus, and her face, sun-blotched and barren, tells us nothing of her mission, but as she wears enormous rollers on her dome she surely had other plans than walking naked through the weeds beneath the noonday sun.

Meanwhile, LITTLE and HALSY have crossed the track and have joined the others, who watch this troubled advance from high in the stands.

We check again the UNDESIRABLES, lately RITA's companions, as they regard with grim good humor her arrival down below.

RITA staggers through the crowd, some of whom ad lib attempts to be jocular. But the freakish is not funny and nakedness is really an affront, an aggression against which there is little defense. Furthermore, her feet are bleeding.

HALSY

(Muttering) Jesus Christ.

RITA reaches a trio of men. She appears to whimper some plea to each of them, but only halfheartedly, as a drunk would, or a panhandler used to being ignored. The men, passing the buck, turn embarrassedly to one another and stand off and blush.

But RITA has hardly waited a moment before moving elsewhere to be declined and this time we are near enough to hear her request.

RITA

Don't you have a blanket?

Again she leaves before the limp Lancelot she addresses can respond, who shrugs red-faced to the crowd; and asks another, who, by way of excuse, calls to his wife: "Honey, do we have any blankets?"

LITTLE

They're going.

HALSY looks to the crest of the hill, to see the UNDESIRABLES depart.

RITA watches them go also. She is to be abandoned now as well as abused, and what is worse, without the authors of her desperation present, she must bear alone the penalties of public outrage.

She stalks across the track in a sudden if tardy mood of indignity and tries the door of the first camper she comes to. It is locked. She goes to the next. A woman and several kids sit in the front seat and the woman rolls up the window at RITA's approach. RITA gestures contemptuously toward the crowd and moves to another vehicle.

RACER

Oh no, not mine. Please stay away from mine.

ANOTHER

(*Up.*) Take mine, baby . . . the Buick!

RACER

She's stoned, man. That chick's on something.

RITA approaches HALSY's pickup.

HALSY

Oh no, oh no.

She opens the door and crawls into the front seat. She lies down and disappears from sight as the door closes after her.

HALSY

Okay, get her out of there.

LITTLE

Me? It's your truck.

HALSY

You're the Good Samaritan.

LITTLE

You're the Don Juan.

ANNOUNCER

(*Loudspeaker*) Riders meeting. All riders start-finish right away. Race starts right away. Riders meeting.

Track and Pits

LITTLE limps in HALSY's wake toward the riders' meeting.

HALSY

Just dump her out, man. Get rid of her. I don't care how.

LITTLE

And just leave her?

HALSY

They did, didn't they?

LITTLE

Yeah, but they're . . . Undesirables.

HALSY

I don't want her in there when I come back, okay? Now I got a bike to ride.

And he joins the other riders assembling around the official at start-finish.

Pickup

LITTLE hobbles without enthusiasm toward the pickup.

At the door he turns back, but he gets no quarter from HALSY. He starts to stand on tiptoe to see into the window, then changes his mind and knocks on the door.

87

> LITTLE

This is our car.

There is no answer. He knocks again. Still no answer. To see into the car he elevates himself as high as he can on his cast.

Pickup Interior

RITA lies along the seat, her face against the leather.

LITTLE's face comes into view in the window.

> LITTLE

Hi, this is our car.

There is no response.

> LITTLE

Do you want a dime or something, to call up somebody?

RITA is not fully conscious.

> RITA

(*Drooling*) The trouble is, I live so far from home.

Pickup Interior

It is night. HALSY is driving. Beside him is RITA, wearing an assortment of men's clothing, and beside her is LITTLE.

RITA still has a glazed, intoxicated look and in fact is being held up by the shoulders of the men on either side of her; a clammy film of sweat is on her brow, and right beneath her aimless glance is terror; from time to time she jerks her head this way and that, trying to ignore the hallucinations that approach around the corners of her eyes.

LITTLE and HALSY are not happy to have her along and already her presence has served to divide them, pushing HALSY into silence and LITTLE into an obliged compensatory protectiveness.

> RITA
> Do you know where a gym is?

> LITTLE
> A gym?

> RITA
> If you come to a town with a gym, just let me out at the gym. I got to start working out.

LITTLE doesn't know what to say.

> HALSY
> She doesn't know what she's talking about. Don't pay any attention.

> RITA
> Who's your friend?

> LITTLE
> You couldn't go to a gym in the middle of the night. There's no gym open in the middle of the night.

> RITA
> Oh, I love that song. What's the name of it?

And she fusses with the radio.

They drive in uneasy silence, RITA having a bad time with herself.

> RITA
> (*Suddenly hold everything, stop the presses.*) Hey, wait a minute. What's your sign, anyway?

> LITTLE
> You mean, my what? When I was born?

> RITA
> What's his?

> LITTLE
> June is all I know. June 8.

> RITA
> Oh no!

> LITTLE
> What's the matter?

> RITA
> Never mind, never mind.

> LITTLE
> Isn't June any good?

> RITA
> Wait a minute, wait a minute. Just tell me where your Mars is. That's all I need to know.

> LITTLE
> I don't know where anything is.

> RITA
> Hell, I hate that song.

She switches the radio off. Nervous time goes by.

RITA

Aren't we anywhere yet? Where the hell are we?
(*Beat.*) Am I in California?

LITTLE

You don't even know where you are at?

HALSY

Leave her alone, Little.

RITA

Where's your Venus? Do you know where your
Venus is?

LITTLE

(*To* HALSY, *nervously*) We going to come to any
gyms?

RITA

Because that's the first thing you do, man, when
you start getting straight, man, is start eating
and putting on fat, man, not me. (*Beat.*) You guys
don't turn on, or what?

LITTLE

You shouldn't ever use that stuff.

RITA

Don't you think I know, don't you think I know!
(*Desperately*) I don't know what to do with my
mind!

LITTLE

What's on the radio . . . anything?

He nervously switches it on.

Because I promised myself I wasn't going to let any more Geminis into my life. They're so *mercurial.*

Restaurant

HALSY, LITTLE and RITA are in a booth in an all-night restaurant on the highway. It has been a silent, nervous meal. A waitress now leaves a check and HALSY reaches for it.

RITA

(*As though to prevent their leaving*) Hey, you don't have a guitar, do you?

LITTLE

A guitar?

RITA

Does he? (*To* HALSY) Do you have a guitar?

HALSY

No, we don't have any guitar.

LITTLE

Do you play a guitar?

RITA

Sure. In New York City I play political guitar and sing for all those phonies.

HALSY stands.

HALSY

You ready?

RITA

Somebody stole my guitar.

Reluctantly, LITTLE stands. HALSY goes off to pay the check.

LITTLE

(*Apologetically*) They'll probably be some gyms open pretty soon. I don't know what time the gyms open.

RITA

No, sure. Listen, don't hang around. Split, it's okay. I don't want you in my Karma anyway. I got to be very careful who I let in my Karma.

LITTLE

Your what?

RITA

Hell, man, I'm going to let nobody in my life when I get straight this time.

HALSY returns with a toothpick in his mouth. He puts a few dollars down before RITA and gives LITTLE a gentle but forceful shove. RITA stares fixedly at the tabletop and the men exit.

Parking Lot

LITTLE and HALSY emerge from the restaurant. They pass a large plate-glass window wherein RITA can be seen sitting alone; LITTLE's attention is divided between RITA's forlorn aspect and HALSY's vigorous effort to remove them from the sway of conscience.

HALSY

Did you ever notice you can drive all day and all night and whenever you stop it's still the same fried eggs served by the same fat waitress and it's like you never went nowhere?

Pickup Interior

They climb into the cab. From where they're parked, RITA is still visible through the restaurant window.

HALSY

You ever notice that?

LITTLE

Yeah. It's like you never went nowhere.

HALSY

That's what I said. Every place is the same.

LITTLE

What's she going to do?

HALSY

That's her lookout.

He starts the engine.

LITTLE

No, wait.

HALSY

What for?

LITTLE

I mean, what's your hurry? Where are we even going?

HALSY

Some other Denny's down the road just like this.

LITTLE

Yeah, just some other Denny's down the road.

HALSY

I gave her five bucks.

LITTLE

You gave her three bucks.

HALSY

Was it three?

LITTLE

What can she do on three dollars?

HALSY

She'll call somebody up.

LITTLE

Long distance. New York or San Francisco. We're here.

HALSY

The big lover.

LITTLE

I'm not the big lover.

HALSY

I knew you'd get yourself in trouble.

LITTLE

You get yourself in trouble, why can't I get myself in trouble?

HALSY

Because I can get myself out again.

Through the windshield and the plate-glass window they watch a waitress clean up before RITA.

LITTLE

I want her.

HALSY

You want her?

LITTLE

I can want a person too, you know.

HALSY

I'll get you somebody. You could have had Moneth.

LITTLE

I want somebody that's mine.

HALSY

That dippy dope head community screw is one of them mamas for all them freaks.

LITTLE

No, man, she's all alone.

Campsite

It is night and the pickup is parked beside a small melodious river. The bike has been removed from the rear of the car and LITTLE, HALSY and RITA have made a bed in its place.

RITA sits up in the corner restlessly smoking but more at peace than before. LITTLE and HALSY lie on their backs looking at the stars, the latter still scowling at this crowded turn of events.

LITTLE

(*Finally*) Do you still get your wish if it's a satellite?

RITA

Do you know what I wish?

HALSY

(*His wish*) I'd just like to win the world and then I'll quit.

RITA

I had a Geiger counter.

HALSY

A Geiger counter?

RITA

I'll marry the first guy comes up with a Geiger counter and we live at the beach. Do you know how much treasure there is just in sand?

LITTLE

Do you know what I wish?

RITA

(*Obliged to ask*) What?

LITTLE

That somebody ask me what I wish.

They take a moment to realize LITTLE's presence is indeed sometimes shadowy.

HALSY

Okay, what do you wish?

LITTLE

(*The impossible*) That we all have good luck and be friends.

Riverside

It is the next morning. HALSY is midstream taking a bath. LITTLE sits on the rocks which line the river; he is pounding his cast with smaller stones and throwing away pieces of plaster. RITA sits nearby, putting on elaborate eye makeup and from time to time evaluating HALSY's scar.

RITA

(*Finally*) How'd he do that?

LITTLE

(*Without looking up at first*) I was going as fast as I had ever went in my whole life and then I fell off.

Now, looking up, he realizes she was asking about HALSY.

LITTLE

Oh—him or me?

RITA

Oh yeah, how'd you break your leg?

LITTLE

(*Obliging what he knows is her real interest*) You remember when Digger was wiped out? He was working on the rigs there.

RITA

Digger?

LITTLE

Isn't it in Oklahoma where the whole town blew up or something?

RITA

Never heard of it.

LITTLE

He wasn't expected to live at first and then he was never expected to walk. I thought it was famous, the way he said.

RITA stares at HALSY midstream.

RITA

(*Doubtfully*) The spine is integrity.

LITTLE removes the final portion of his cast and regards his shriveled unappealing calf and ankle.

LITTLE

(*After a moment*) What's the leg?

RITA

The leg? (*She thinks.*) The leg's support.

Riders' Meeting

It is a bright breezy Sunday afternoon. As usual, a great number of pickups and trucks line the inside of the track, while the spectators in the dilapidated stands are few.

Near start-finish, a riders' meeting is in progress, racers grouped around an OFFICIAL.

OFFICIAL

And all you tuners and sponsors got to conform too, with no more weird outfits in the pits. Because we're seeing too many weird outfits in the pits.

In the group surrounding the OFFICIAL, we spot HALSY leathered for a race and wearing an African safari hat; and LITTLE picking his neck and yawning as his attention strays to the pickup in the vicinity and, as we shall see, RITA; and a couple of dozen other faces of varying attention and interest.

RICK NIFTY is among this number, a championship racer distinguished by the seasoned mechanics surrounding him and the deferential side glances of the other riders, particularly HALSY, who maneuvers through the crowd for more advantageous proximity.

OFFICIAL

You all want to keep racing something you can be proud of, don't you, in the public mind and not mixed up, which it is in most people's minds, with these other bike clubs which will remain unmentionable . . .

HALSY mumbles his gruff commitment to this cause in an effort to attract RICK NIFTY's attention, if not his approval, and other riders react enthusiastically as well, with pimpled pride. Some even choke on their hotdogs and packaged pies, so stirred are they by this stimulating pep talk.

OFFICIAL

. . . which is entirely up to you guys, the public opinion you want to give to get rid of in the public mind that everybody rides motorcycles is a bunch of bums . . .

Pan with LITTLE as he departs the riders' meeting for the snack shack and favoring his weak leg passes through a milling crowd, which unfortunately only confirms the image the fading official above is trying to refute.

Snack Shack

LITTLE waits in line at the snack shack.

> ANNOUNCER
> (*Loudspeaker crossfading with* OFFICIAL) There's beer and soft drinks over here in the snack shack, folks, for all of you who'd like to gloat yourself before the big race begins, is this damn sound on, Joe? Can you hear me down there? It ain't working, or is it? I ain't talking just to hear myself . . .

LITTLE crosses to the pickup with two soft drinks.

> ANNOUNCER
> (*Blaring*) Testing: one, two, three, damnit!

Pickup

RITA sits in a camp chair in the rear-truck part of the pickup, a portable umbrella fastened over her head. She is reading compulsively, as she has been, we assume, non-stop for days.

> LITTLE
> You want a pop?

She doesn't look up from her book.

RITA

Not me, man. That stuff's poison.

LITTLE

I just thought you might be getting hot or something.

RITA

If I get hot, I'll tell you.

LITTLE

I mean thirsty.

She sets her book down angrily.

RITA

Do you know how many underprivileged countries are hooked on United States pop?

LITTLE

All it is is sugar.

RITA

(*Accusingly*) Sugar, yeah!

LITTLE

What's the matter with sugar?

RITA

It poses as love!

And she resumes with her book.

LITTLE waits a minute. Then:

LITTLE

Would you want a hot dog or anything?

RITA slams the book down in her lap and stares at LITTLE. He smiles back without the sense to know his life's in danger.

The riders' meeting adjourned, RICK NIFTY heads back to his bike, HALSY at his heels.

> HALSY
>
> Well, I see there's a lot of illustrious people here today . . .

He overtakes the celebrity and assaults him with an eager handshake.

> HALSY
>
> You probably don't remember, but a couple years back before the Army had me for two years and I got this back messed up, me and you went around together at the Nationals at Daytona.

RICK NIFTY immediately recognizes the phony and pretender in HALSY, but his position as hero requires some tolerance.

> RICK NIFTY
>
> That right?

He smiles faintly and the best he can do to protect himself is continue on toward his crew.

But HALSY keeps up.

> HALSY
>
> Well, you have went on to be pretty illustrious and I was, like I say, called into the Army for two years where my back was messed up and—

> RICK NIFTY
>
> This your home town?

103

HALSY

This burg? You kidding? One thing I can say about this track is, if you go off course, you'll never know it.

RICK NIFTY

They ought to pave it or sweep it at least when it gets that gravelly.

HALSY

Well, when Uncle Sam calls you got to do your duty and you do your duty even when it costs you you got to begin all over again. I see you're still with Kawasaki.

RICK NIFTY

We're trying out a new 250 here looks pretty good.

HALSY

Say, I wanted to ask you, how do you get to sit on a tank like that? It's who you know, huh?

There is no answer as they continue across the pits, RICK NIFTY too shiny to be sucked into any low-grade camaraderie.

HALSY

I been thinking of going factory-sponsored myself.

RICK NIFTY

Well, looks like I better get to work if I'm going to do any racing today.

They have arrived at the Kawasaki setup.

HALSY

Oh, sure, I just wanted to extend my apologies

for this rotten track and tell you just watch out for all that transmission fluid and grease spots they left us from the drag races last night and a . . .

He offers his hand again several times, but it goes unnoticed as RICK NIFTY is suddenly preoccupied with his bike.

HALSY

And a . . . I just wanted you to know it's a real pleasure to have such a top professional go-faster here today to go around with, and maybe I'll see you down at Daytona again this year. Oh, by the way, when is Daytona this year?

RICK NIFTY takes HALSY's hand briefly, once and for all brushing him off.

RICK NIFTY

Same here. Thanks a lot.

Cut to Start-Finish

Close shot on HALSY's eyes through the visor of his helmet. They are narrowed, filled with hate.

Pull back enough to see the object of this emotion, RICK NIFTY in the row ahead.

The flag whips through the air and the race is on, the first heat in this class.

Little's Vantage

LITTLE stands on the top of the pickup and watches the race. Not so RITA, who sits in the truck below reading, her ears plugged against the roar or any other interruption.

Announcer's Tower

HALSY's struggle to win is dramatized by the ANNOUNCER's garbled commentary, no word of which, however, is recognizable.

First Heat

We ride with HALSY as he tries to overtake RICK NIFTY.

Start-Finish

HALSY makes impressive gains and falls short of winning only by a few lengths.

Pits

Dancing energetically around the bike, HALSY splits open his leathers and ties them around his waist as LITTLE crouches down to the engine to make adjustments. Behind them in the pickup, RITA reads on.

> HALSY
> I was in that sucker's draft the whole time around from the back straight. Did you see him cut back and forth?

> LITTLE
> (*Mumbling to himself*) If I got juice here, then I got to have juice here, so all it could be is, no, wait a minute.

> HALSY
> That ain't even legal, I got him so panicked.

LITTLE

Halsy, will you hold the damn bike, for heck sake!

HALSY obliges.

HALSY

(*Vowing to win*) He just better watch his ass this time.

LITTLE

You just better watch yours.

HALSY surveys the sparse grandstand.

HALSY

What they ought to do is pay me extra for making it interesting. That's what those square johns want to see is real muscle fighting it out. (*Fired by his own propaganda*) Two top go-fast guys fighting it out to the finish!

RITA

(*Sarcastic*) The World! Starring Halsy Knox!

HALSY

Did you say something, Lady Godiva?

LITTLE

(*Stumped*) Who knows anything about condensers?

Start-Finish

Fewer racers this time, and HALSY is next to RICK NIFTY. It is the final. Pre-start tension is high. The flag is up. It's down. The bikes charge down the straight.

All but HALSY's, which won't start. He pushes it at a run, but to no avail. LITTLE rushes onto the track to help, but they cannot get enough momentum to ignite the engine.

HALSY drops the bike and stamps around in anguished tantrum, gesturing accusations at LITTLE and all but kicking the bike. LITTLE blushes at this display before the grandstands.

Pickup Interior

RITA reads by flashlight as the three drive through the night again.

> HALSY
> (*Still fuming*) No Scott Roddy Rick Nifty Van Dusen Jim Dandy Sinclair's going to lift his leg on me and get away with it.

Involuntarily, LITTLE and RITA exchange a subtle look of boredom.

> HALSY
> That bastard think he's the only one ever made Daytona?

> LITTLE
> When were you at Daytona, Hals?

> HALSY
> He don't know I wasn't never at Daytona.

Moody silence.

HALSY

It rained the year I went to Daytona. I drove all the way to Daytona and then it rained.

LITTLE

They race rain or shine at Daytona, I always thought.

HALSY

(*After a minute*) Not during hurricanes they don't. It was during hurricane I think Esther and all of Florida was closed.

Again, LITTLE and RITA share a look. This time HALSY catches them and it adds to his temper.

HALSY

Who the hell couldn't win a race they fly in in the morning and fly out at night with the top tuners working on the top bikes for you?

LITTLE

(*Losing patience*) You carried your mad into the race with you, Halsy. Which is the dumbest thing anybody can do if they want to win a race . . .

HALSY

No, I got to get me a sponsor . . .

LITTLE

And that's why you goofed up. You carried your mad with you.

HALSY

Somebody *knows* bikes. At least condensers.

RITA puts aside her book as tempers heat the cab.

LITTLE

Man, that condenser was fine.

HALSY

I can't get nowhere on that Mickey Mouse scooter
you got, Little.

LITTLE

You flooded it, that's why you goofed up. You
can't ride!

RITA switches on the radio. HALSY switches it off before
it even warms up. LITTLE reaches up and switches it
on again. They all stare ahead at the road but their
minds are roaring. A vocal fades in on the radio, Tammy
Wynette singing the country Western tune "Divorce."

Raceway

It is a Sunday midafternoon and this is a Le Mans
start. The bikes are on one side of the track, the racers
on the other. LITTLE holds HALSY's bike for him. The
song begun at the end of the previous scene continues.

The flag is down. The racers run across the track and
grab their bikes and with varied fortune they are down
the front straight.

We travel with HALSY to a minor spill at the far turn,
cutting away at the moment of the accident to:

Pickup

On the blanket in the shade by the pickup, LITTLE and
RITA sit in the lotus position, she more expert than he.

110

He is trying to roll his eyes inward and she is trying to adjust his limbs to their proper spiritual mingling, betweentimes blowing on a mouth harp and spinning a prayer wheel and referring to a master volume in her lap, and all the while trying to remain in position herself.

The song "Divorce" continues, though not so loud as to drown out the announcement "Rider down," and in the background people in the pits have reacted with concern to the accident, some even running toward the disastrous turn. Not so LITTLE and RITA, who are oblivious of all but their devotions.

Infield

His leathers torn and covered with dust, HALSY pushes his wounded bike back to the pits. The inside of his visor is smeared with blood.

Pickup

Unfortunately, LITTLE and RITA are standing on their heads when HALSY arrives. He looks down at them, his wound more unsightly than critical, but nonetheless accusing.

They stare back at him upsidedown, while Tammy Wynette sings on.

Close shot on a guilty LITTLE upsidedown. Then *spin around* to

Roadhouse

Close shot right side up on LITTLE, angry and envious, abetted by booze.

Pull back to reveal a dim dance floor surrounded by small tables decorated with beer bottles, and LITTLE alone, watching HALSY and RITA dance. On the bandstand is a small family group of country musicians, featuring the vocal talents of a twelve-year-old daughter in mascara and bubble-do, singing the Tammy Wynette arrangement of "Divorce."

HALSY's manner of dancing is rather curious. His hands and arms are placed around RITA in such a way as to suggest that he carries a heavy log or totem pole, and he weaves this way and that in a kind of showy romantic expertise that reminds one of the polka and the Balboa and threatens any moment to floor him.

We remain with this sequence to the conclusion of the song begun in the earlier scene, studying the sated child-woman who sings of divorce, RITA listless and used, if not a little seasick in HALSY's arms; LITTLE jealous and enraged but muted in booze; and finally HALSY, whose exaggerated aplomb intends perhaps to be disruptive and threatening and is at the core vengeful and deadly.

Wet with sweat and sighing with rather too generous exhalations of animal accomplishment, HALSY sinks back into his chair when the song ends. He examines the beer bottles, now empty on the table, as RITA, straight-backed and remote, sits down also.

HALSY
Drinking up all the old beer, old buddy?

Without answering, LITTLE gets to his feet and crosses the dance floor to the bandstand as though to make a request before he throws up.

HALSY

(*To* RITA) Want another beer?

RITA

(*Her way of declining*) I guess you haven't read the statistics on alcoholism in the United States lately.

HALSY

(*Swacked*) Like me, huh? Got a champagne taste but a beer appetite.

He waves for the waitress as the music begins again.

RITA

See if they have any sunflower seeds and honey. Or baklavah.

She has hardly finished her sentence, however, when her attention, along with HALSY's, is drawn to the dance floor, where a drunken LITTLE is dancing wildly with the child chanteuse. So frenzied is his footwork that it tells us all and even HALSY and RITA that someone has been dancing on his heart.

Flat Tire

Somewhere on the highway the pickup has a flat tire and LITTLE is changing it. HALSY sits under a tree nearby, and RITA is in evidence only by her bare feet, which stick out of the cab window. (She is lying along the front seat, we presume, reading.) Each man is rather hung over and diesel trucks roaring past now and then jar them seriously.

LITTLE

(*As he works*) Halsy . . . ?

HALSY

Whatee?

LITTLE

Whatee?

HALSY

(*Blushing*) Never mind. What?

LITTLE

What's *whatee?*

HALSY

Never mind, damnit. What did you want? Didn't you ever say whatee when somebody said your name?

LITTLE

I just want to tell you something.

HALSY

Okay what?

LITTLE looks up at the bare feet extended from the window and then proceeds with his work.

LITTLE

What I was wondering was when your suspension's up.

HALSY

What are you, homesick? If you're homesick, go home if you want.

LITTLE

I want my bike back and my license. I want to be Little again and you be Halsy.

HALSY gets agitatedly to his feet.

> HALSY
>
> Sure, man, screw it. Right away. I don't give a damn.

> LITTLE
>
> You don't have to be dragged.

> HALSY
>
> They'll cancel my suspension soon as I pay my dues. And I'm in business. Don't worry about me.

> LITTLE
>
> It's just my leg's better, that's all.

> HALSY
>
> Who says I'm dragged? I'm not dragged.

> LITTLE
>
> Then would you hand me them bolts?

HALSY scowls at the bare feet and crossed ankles coming out of the window.

> HALSY
>
> Only tell it true. It's not your gimpy leg you want to exercise.

> LITTLE
>
> I want to race, that's all.

> HALSY
>
> It's your bike and you race it. Only don't tell me it's your bike you want to race.

> LITTLE
>
> What do I want, then?

HALSY

You want the chick.

LITTLE

Well?

He looks at RITA's feet and slowly stands.

LITTLE

She's not your chick.

HALSY

She's sure as hell not your chick.

The diesels are roaring past thick and fast now, adding to the fury of the moment.

LITTLE

It was my idea to take her along.

HALSY

Yeah, but whose truck is it?

LITTLE

Well, it's your truck, but it's winning on my bike's paying for food and gas.

HALSY

I'm breaking my ass to give you points and you're trying to take my chick away from me.

Now there are no diesels and it is suddenly quiet.

LITTLE

(*Still shouting*) You're trying to take my chick away from *me!*

HALSY withdraws and assumes a martyred pose against the tree.

116

HALSY

If that's friendship, I'm aghast.

LITTLE goes back to working on the tire.

LITTLE

I never said I was your friend, Halsy. (*And then:*)
In fact, I don't even like you.

HALSY

Well, so he blurted it out!

LITTLE

I'm not even blurting it. I'm telling you cool and
cold I don't like you and I never did and anything
I ever had to say to you I had to think up.

HALSY

(*Now angry too*) If we're going to settle this,
Little, without I hit you in the face, I guess
we better call Rita out here and see where she
stands.

LITTLE looks up nervously to the bare feet, one scratching
the other thoughtfully.

Longshot

We see the pickup pull from the soft shoulder in a
cloud of dust.

Pickup Interior

Eyes narrowed in anger, HALSY guns the engine forward.
He is alone in the cab.

Highway

Astride his bike, LITTLE stares after the pickup swathed in the dust of its departure.

Rear of Pickup

Wind whips hair around RITA's plaintive squint as she tries to read and not look back.

Highway

The pickup now out of sight, LITTLE shoves the pedal down furiously. The engine fails to start for some time, increasing his lonely plight. Finally it catches and he revs the motor with mounting roar. Behind his glasses we see tears and feel the velocity of his engine is an amplification of this pain. But before he succumbs to it totally, he whips onto the highway and begins almost immediately to shrink into the distance.

When the sound of his motor has diminished sufficiently:

> SEALLY
> (*Voice over*) You were a fool, Little.

Seally's Bedroom

SEALLY FAUSS isn't well. One glance at him propped against his pillows tells us time is soon to run out on him. His bones protrude and he is ashen. But that is all there is to be said about his illness, except for a flicker of fear and panicky good will seen now and then in MOM.

MOM and LITTLE sit at the foot of his bed, their feet up. LITTLE's face is clean but marked by the sun in the shape of goggles, and even now the sound of his journey is still receding.

LITTLE is looking at snapshots—those we recognize taken by the PHOTOGRAPHER and developed since by SEALLY from the stolen camera HALSY left behind.

LITTLE

Don't feel no better about it with proof.

MOM

For all we know he could of committed foul play to come by that camera, Little, and they'd of took you as accomplish.

LITTLE

He don't need to get rough, old Halsy. Long as nobody ever speaks up and says hey man, you ain't told the truth. That's what he's got going, that nobody ever says that ain't what you said yesterday.

Motel Room

HALSY lies stomach down on the bed while RITA, propped up on her elbows, studies, as though it were the eighth wonder of the world, the scar that runs along his lower spine.

HALSY

(*There is something in his mood which suggests he might be telling the truth this time, though*

that something is always there with the gifted liar.)
I just as soon as died and half the time I thought
I did already and I'd have conversations with
the other bodies. Are you dead? And they'd say,
oh yeah, are you—and by the time I knew I
wasn't, they'd bored two holes in my head and
was pulling my head in one direction and my
feet in the other and turning me every half hour
like a barbecued chicken on a spit to keep my
poor old spine from sagging.

RITA

(*Won't believe him.*) People die with broken backs.

But she leans down to run her tongue along the cruel
cuneiform that parallels his spine.

HALSY

Usually people die, but a lot of times things happen
that aren't usual. Sometimes a person falls twelve
stories and doesn't die. And I fell down five steps
and broke my neck.

RITA

You broke your back, dummy. If you broke your
neck, you'd have to be dead.

HALSY rolls over to look at her.

HALSY

(*Accusing*) And all because of some dumb broad
named Bunny.

RITA

(*Holding him off*) Listen, my name is Rita Nebraska and not Bunny, and I got scars too. So
don't take your shit out on me.

HALSY

What scars have you got?

RITA

I got this whole beautiful brilliant family, man, I love and I been on the streets since fifteen years old. And I mean Europe too, and *cobblestones*. And I can't never go back to them.

HALSY

You ain't got no scars, Rita. You're just fat.

RITA

(*After a hurt moment*) Bunny must really been mean.

HALSY

Just your average whore. Only I was just out of high school and all it seemed to me was she was fast. But that's what I was too, so I had big plans, and I knew if I could get her to Recreation Park I could lay her.

RITA

Recreation Park! Did you have a Recreation Park?

HALSY

It was hot and I was running around from the bathroom to the bedroom and twisting and turning back and forth looking sideways at myself in the mirro' and smelling my armpit and must of all the excitement of the big date, I don't know, made me dizzy. Because all I remember is at the bottom of the stairs turning around to go back for something. A handkerchief or brush my teeth or something. And must of I made it to the top of the stairs in two leaps because the next thing I know I'm in intensive care for a month on that spit and then three months in a complete body cast. And all I got from Bunny Patchen was this get-well card saying it's better this way, Halsy, because it could never work out due to what you place so much importance on and I don't.

RITA
(*Waiting for this opening*) I know. The same thing happened to me——

HALSY
The same thing didn't happen to you, damnit! It happened to me, not to you!

RITA
No what I mean is you wanted to be responded to. It's universal. I'm looking for my salvation too. We're all looking for our salvations. You're not at peace. I know the feeling.

HALSY
Bullshit.

RITA
It's called moving off your center. We are all looking for our centers.

HALSY
If I'd told you I was tortured by wild Persian tribes while I went around the world for UPA, you'd have listened. But I told you the truth and you weren't even listening, so what good is the truth?

And he stares into the gloom unexpressed and unreceived and distantly a quiet bike appears as a slow *crossfade* begins.

Country Lane

Here is a leafy country road, and moving down it silently beneath the speckled sunlight and shadow, is LITTLE, riding the rear wheel of his bike. This is a soundless ballet of longing and loneliness.

The Beach

Seabirds ride the breezes of a gloomy day. On the all but deserted sand, RITA is bundled into several sweaters and hats and kerchiefs as she slowly moves her Geiger counter back and forth over the surface of the sand, checking the meter industriously. Shirtless and shivering and wearing a cowboy hat, HALSY has trouble keeping his pace as slow as hers as she listens through heavy earphones for El Dorado. His patience runs out and he circles around to confront her.

> HALSY
>
> You asked me where my Mars was and kept on bugging me about my Mars and when I told you where my Mars was you come up with where's my Venus.

> RITA
>
> Sh-sh-sh, will you please? Be quiet.

> HALSY
>
> What am I making it, nervous?

RITA

You're moving me very off my center today, Halsy,
if you don't mind.

He grabs her arm so that she must stop her prospecting.

HALSY

I don't know where your center is, Rita, and
I don't know where my planets are. But I do
know we're broke and if you don't come up with
more than bottle caps and pennies today I'm going
to hock that toy.

RITA

Hock your own toy, Halsy. You don't hock mine.

And she shakes loose.

HALSY

(*Stunned*) Hock my bike?

RITA

What good is it? You ain't made dime one since
you went a hundred percent. Which if you ask
me ought to tell you something.

HALSY

Okay, what? Ought to tell me what?

RITA

You need Little.

And she moves on, waving her gadget over the sand.

Countryside

Helmeted and fighting LITTLE shoots down a dirt road
on his bike; he makes a rough turn and then tears

up another straight, this time as though to an imaginary finish.

On a faint rise he slows to a stop. If the earlier scene of him riding alone was wistful and balletic, he is now someone preparing for ultimate achievement and complete mastery of his sport.

He removes his helmet and checks a stopwatch he has on a string around his neck, his lips mumbling some excited liturgy.

Then something in the distance catches his eye and he squints through his smudged glasses down the fields toward his home.

Fauss's Yard

MOM waves a black flag toward the distant hillside where LITTLE practices. Her expression is one of worry and concern. She stops waving the flag when she sees LITTLE's dust cloud approaching.

LITTLE rides into the yard and removes his helmet.

>   LITTLE
> What's the matter?

>   MOM
> (*Darkly*) Sideburns is here.

If LITTLE reacts, it is imperceptible.

Dirt Road

HALSY and LITTLE, the latter carrying a large can of gas, walk down the dirt road leading from the Fauss house.

125

(*Tightly*) You took some chance, coming all the
way out here on a empty tank.

HALSY

You might have let me starve, but I know you'd
never let any motor go hungry.

An extended silence follows this effort to be friendly.

HALSY

(*Trying hard*) I was real sorry to hear about
your father, Little. I always liked the old gentle-
man.

LITTLE

(*Unbending*) More'n he had to say for you.

HALSY

No, I was much shocked to hear of his untimely
domain.

Another Angle

To include the pickup down the road at an odd angle
where it has run out of gas. As we near, RITA can
be seen in the front seat.

LITTLE

What is it you want, Halsy?

HALSY

(*Having difficulty*) Boy, you're mean, Little. Shoot.
You don't respond to people. That's a bad trait.
People want to be responded to. Like I have
to bend over backwards just to catch your eyes.

Pickup

They approach RITA framed in the passenger window.

> HALSY
>
> I said to Rita, this is going to be a tough re-union with Little, but damn it all, worth it.

> LITTLE
>
> How are you, Rita?

> RITA
>
> I'm fine, Little. How are you?

> LITTLE
>
> Just fine, thank you.

And there being nothing more to say, LITTLE goes to the rear of the truck and removes the gas cap.

HALSY stands by as LITTLE gases the car. Then he pulls a tarpaulin off the rear of the pickup and reveals a cycle and sidehack mounted there.

> LITTLE
>
> Where'd you get that?

> HALSY
>
> I was wondering when the heck you'd notice.

> LITTLE
>
> You racing sidehack now, huh? Who with?

> HALSY
>
> Jimmy Fast got killed at Rialta, I don't know if you knew. And his old lady said take it, she never wanted to see it again.

> LITTLE
>
> What about Herrera?

HALSY

I gave him Rita's Geiger counter for his half.

LITTLE

No, I mean he okay?

HALSY

He's going to be all right but he don't have no nose.

LITTLE

Well, who you hacking *with,* then?

HALSY gives vent to a dazzling but still thin and uncertain smile.

HALSY

Well, I hope my old friend Little Fauss from Columbine.

The moment is ripe for reunion, but the car door slams and RITA comes into view.

RITA

Half that thing's mine tell him. My Geiger counter bought it.

She is big with child and LITTLE looks at her, stunned. She stops in her tracks and looks at HALSY as though to say: Didn't you tell him? HALSY looks at LITTLE and shrugs innocently. LITTLE puts the gas cap back on and screws it tight.

Dirt Road

LITTLE strides back up the road toward his house, HALSY in his wake.

128

HALSY

(*Time running out.*) We couldn't hustle up enough loot soon enough to hustle up some doctor, and now it's too late and . . .

He has to increase his speed to keep up with LITTLE.

HALSY

Hell, I'd marry her like that only they just caught up with me for nonsupport on one family. Ask Rita. We had to skip out fast. And hell I don't even know if I'm even divorced yet. And hell you know me, I'm not the kind of guy can just cut out on a girl. And so, remembering how much in love you two were, I figured I would step out politely of your ways if you just thought you might want to team up again.

LITTLE

You mean come on back and be your tuner and take a crack at Rita now and then if I want to, huh?

HALSY

What a low mind you have, Little.

LITTLE

You just want to dump her on me, man.

HALSY

I knew you'd think that.

LITTLE

Because that's how it is.

HALSY

For all I know it's your kid.

LITTLE

It's not my kid.

HALSY

It's not I even mind it's not my kid but she can't even tell me whose kid it is.

LITTLE

More'n one most likely of them unmentionables.

HALSY

Who I'll have to bring it up!

LITTLE

Well, I ain't bringing it up.

Fauss's Yard

LITTLE is about to turn into the yard, when HALSY gets in his path.

HALSY

(*Confidentially*) It'd break my heart to have to give up Rita, but if that's what I have to do——

LITTLE

Don't do nothing for me, Hals.

HALSY

Little, I need you.

LITTLE

I ain't no tuner no more. I race.

HALSY

I want you to race. That's what I'm here for I need you to race sidehack for me.

LITTLE

I ain't climbing on no sidehack just to hold you down, Halsy.

HALSY

Promoters in California pay you just for showing up if you race sidehack.

LITTLE

I race solo. A hundred percent.

HALSY

(*Positive that such simple truth must be persuasive*) She's having a baby, man, and I don't have a dime.

LITTLE

(*After a moment*) I'm going to Daytona.

HALSY

(*Stunned*) Daytona?

LITTLE

Yeah, that's all I'm going to do. I ain't racing sidehack. I ain't getting screwed up again. I'm just going to race Daytona. And screw people.

He turns and leaves HALSY and goes into the house. HALSY stares after him, eyes narrowed.

Take time with HALSY's reaction. A great deal is happening for him: hurt, anger, challenge and finally an understanding guilt that perhaps he created the LITTLE he just now saw barren and unforgiving.

In the meantime, tired of waiting, RITA has brought the pickup up the road to the Fauss gate. It stops behind HALSY and in a moment he gets into the passenger side.

Pickup

It is night and RITA is driving. HALSY sits beside her, head back against the seat. He is wide awake and thinking and one suspects there has been little conversation for some time. Finally:

> HALSY
>
> Hey.

> RITA
>
> Yeah?

But he says nothing.

> RITA
>
> Well?

> HALSY
>
> I make it a rule never to make any promises.

> RITA
>
> So?

> HALSY
>
> I just want you to know, though, you can count on me.

> RITA
>
> (*After a moment*) I make it a rule never to count on no one.

> HALSY
>
> Good. Then maybe we'll get along.

They drive on in silence that is snug and trustful.

132

Little's Bedroom

It is dark but there is light enough from the moon to see that LITTLE is awake and staring at the cold and silent glowing bulk of his bike beside the bed. It seems a monstrous partner in this chilly light.

The sound of racing has begun and it builds loudly as we *hold* on this fierce machine, for the moment stilled.

California Night TT

Paralleling the front straight here is a mound of earth serving as a jump, or what is called steeple chase. One by one, riders fly into the air over this and we *freeze frame* on each until LITTLE and then we move in for a grainy *closeup* of his mad inflight concentration.

In the same manner we drop each back into the race and go with LITTLE as he grinds around a turn, inching ahead of another racer.

Raceway Day

Another time, another place, and HALSY and his new partner, WALLY JAY, and five other sidehacks come out of a turn and spread out down the straight.

California Night TT

Reverse angle as LITTLE and other TT racers come into the straight.

Raceway Day

We travel with HALSY and WALLY JAY down the straight, WALLY JAY lying flat, his nose inches above the track.

Then WALLY JAY moves up and leans on the wind far to the right as the sidehack goes into another curve.

California Night TT

LITTLE pivots on his skidshoe through another curve, then twists and thrusts forward around his nearest rival.

Raceway Day

WALLY JAY scrambles over HALSY to give weight to the left of the bike as HALSY negotiates the final turn into the front straight.

HALSY bears down on the controls to move on the lead racer.

California Night TT

LITTLE bullets down against the fence to get the checkered flag of first place.

Raceway Day

The flag snaps through the air with HALSY and WALLY JAY clearly in first place as the loudspeaker confirms this good fortune.

But the hack doesn't seem to slow down and as soon as it can, it turns rapidly into the pits and as though still racing bumps over the rough ground toward the pickup.

Pickup

The door is open and RITA stands on the running board wearing a t-shirt which advertises Yamaha and which she twists and pulls nervously down over her enormous belly. Her time has come and she is frightened.

HALSY jumps off his bike and hurries toward her as WALLY JAY begins immediate preparations for loading the bike onto the trailer.

> RITA
> Just shut up and hurry up.

> HALSY
> You okay?

RITA grabs his arm as he hurries out of his leathers.

> RITA
> (*Scared to death*) Halsy, first aid and a big smile is not going to get me through this.

> HALSY
> (*Weak and uneasy*) Boy, what a prima donna.

> RITA
> You're supposed to practice and exercise and take breathing lessons and everything and hell I've goofed up again—(*The first contraction.*) I'm not ready!

HALSY gets free of her and turns to WALLY JAY, who is trying to get the bike onto the trailer, not an easy job for one person.

> HALSY
> You hang around and pick up the dough, okay?

135

What are you going to do?

But already HALSY is running toward the ambulance, which is a standard feature at these races.

California Night TT

LITTLE, ablaze with embarrassment, sits on his bike in the bright lights before the grandstand. A miniskirted, false-eyelashed, middle-aged professional trophy girl kisses his cheek and a broad-bellied, ten-gallon-hatted race promoter limply shakes his hand for the benefit of several crouched photographers who flash a few obliged shots. Then all drift off disinterestedly, the photographer, the promoter and the trophy girl, and leave LITTLE squinting into the grandstand, where the crowd is already heading for home or at least another beer.

Ambulance Interior

HALSY sits beside a prone and pain-racked RITA as the ambulance races down a daylit freeway.

> RITA
> (*As though she faced death*) I want someone to call my father.

> HALSY
> (*Strong*) No one needs to call your father, baby. I'm right here, I'm your father.

RITA takes a fevered moment to hold onto this and finds that it is firm and reliable, and her desperation relaxes accordingly.

RITA

(*Lighter mood*) If we do go to Florida, that's where they winter. I could call them up and really blow their minds.

HALSY

We're going to go to Florida, baby. And you're going to blow your old man's mind and I'm going to win the old Two Hundred.

She holds tightly to his hand and strength flows back and forth between them.

RITA

If I live.

California Night TT

It is late and almost everyone has left. LITTLE, his bike already on the truck we saw earlier, transporting Portable Potties, has changed to his street clothes and just now finishes packing his tools away.

There is a strong feeling of letdown and loneliness in the vast unpeopled park as the overhead lights are, section by section, switched off. Across the track, a light remains on in the snack shack at the top of the stands, empty but for attendants sweeping.

LITTLE crosses the track and goes through the gate to the stands. He stops. A GIRL sits in the shadows halfway up. The light is behind her, outlining her shape and hair; something about her is familiar and she appears to be waiting for him.

LITTLE

Rita?

The GIRL stands and LITTLE approaches her uncertainly, almost as if she were a ghost.

Snack Shack

Alas, it is not RITA but rather MONETH (GIRL 2) and she and LITTLE stand before the snack shack now as it closes up and try to drink steaming coffee and have nothing to say to each other but look around in the darkness, embarrassed, for the one that unites them but isn't there.

Moneth's Bedroom

Close shot on LITTLE and MONETH in the throes of passion, their brows filmy, their eyes glazed.

> MONETH
> (*Thick and breathless*) What have you heard from——oh? What have you heard from——ah? What have you heard from–oh–ah–Halsy, anything?

LITTLE stops. He remains in position but the mood has flown. He stares at the sheet inches away from his eyes.

> LITTLE
> (*Finally*) Knocked up some whore there a while back. Probably had to get married by now.

MONETH reaches disappointedly for a pack of cigarettes.

> MONETH
> Just have a smoke, honey. You'll be okay.

Hospital Waiting Room

Stage the cliché. HALSY sits in the muggy atmosphere of many cigarettes, staring at the floor.

A formidable NURSE comes to the door.

> NURSE
>
> Are you Mr. Knox?

HALSY gets slowly to his feet.

> HALSY
>
> (*Terrified*) Why?

> NURSE
>
> Your wife, Miss Nebraska, has just been delivered of a healthy, six-pound, infant girl. (*Quoting distastefully*) She's asking to see you . . . if you haven't split.

Moneth's Bedroom

It is morning and LITTLE falls naked to the floor with a loud noise.

Sitting up, he looks back to the bed to see MONETH's nude leg extending from under the sheet. Tied to her toe is a string which reaches to his ankle and it is this that has floored him as he moved stealthily from her side.

MONETH is also awake now and sitting up.

> MONETH
>
> (*Angry*) You guys. You can't even say goodbye and thank you.

LITTLE

I was going to say goodbye and thank you. But
not if you broke my leg. With Daytona coming up.

He gets to his feet and starts to dress.

MONETH

Yeah, and if you see your boyfriend down there
tell him for me he taught you all the wrong things.

The arrow hits its mark and LITTLE pauses momentarily as
he dresses.

MONETH

Because you sure both sure like to leave a woman
high and dry.

LITTLE

Could be you, you know.

MONETH

Me?

LITTLE

(*Angry*) And don't you you guys me, Moneth.
I'm me.

MONETH

Maybe you used to be but you're sure not now.

LITTLE

Because me and Halsy ain't even friends any more.
Much less what you say . . . *boyfriends.*

Nude and repentant, MONETH flies from the bed to his arms.

MONETH

Just say goodbye. That's all I ask!

He disengages her with difficulty.

LITTLE
Goodbye, Moneth!

Truck Interior

LITTLE is at the wheel, squinting at the road ahead through busy windshield wipers.

HALSY
(*Voice over, reciting*)
Daytona Speedweek, you oval beguiler,
I long to enter your Two Hundred Miler.

Truck Exterior

Heavy rain dashes on LITTLE's bike secured in the rear of the truck.

HALSY
(*Voice over, continued*)
And lest I forget, though it's needless to mention,
Your Armory Trade Show commands my attention.

Pickup Exterior

The same rain falls on HALSY's bright new bike as the pickup speeds down a Southern highway.

HALSY
(*Voice over, continued*)
Good to see Goodyear and Honda and Harley,

141

And Nixon and Bauman and Tanner and
   Charlie . . .

Pickup Interior

RITA drives through the heavy rain. In the passenger seat
HALSY, wearing a Russian fur hat, cradles a sleeping
infant and reads from several scraps of paper he holds
in his free hand.

                    HALSY
   Top hotshoes and go-fasters racing together
   In spite of the cocksucking Florida weather.

                    RITA
   They'll never print that.

                    HALSY
   Oh yeah. They printed all them stories and articles
   of how I cycled through South America.

                    RITA
   (*Patiently*) India.

                    HALSY
   What?

                    RITA
   You said it was India you cycled through, not
   South America.

                    HALSY
   Did I say India? That's right, India. That's where
   it was. Turkey. Turkistan. All them places. Burma.
   India.

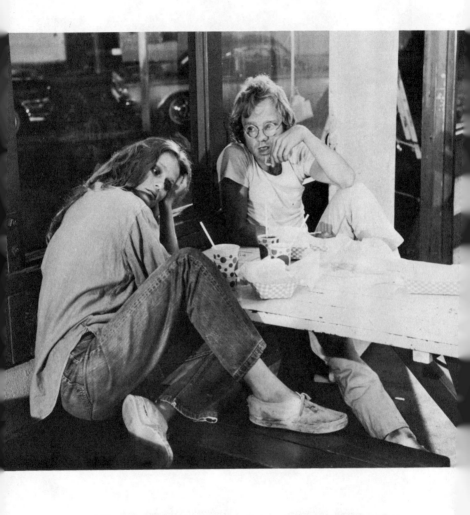

Sunny Florida

This stretch of highway parallels a bright beach with gleaming winter's surf. It seems every car that passes is a pickup or a trailer truck and each transports a shining cycle, and some several.

Daytona Raceway

The stands and snack shops are empty, but the entrances to the parking area are clogged with trucks and pickups heaped with bikes brilliant in the noonday sun. This is the first day of registration.

> HALSY
> (*Voice over, reciting*)
> You're never the same, once Big "D" has got you,
> For here's where the little guy knocks out the hotshoe.

The raceway office overflows with riders and mechanics and officials, while outside, teams huddle together in serious groups, looking at their feet.

> HALSY
> (*Voice over*)
> Here's where they go round and farewell to routine,
> Convincing America bikes can be clean.

Wives and children hover uncertainly in the background, staring out of pickups and camper windows, tired and anxious to move on to whatever quarters will be theirs during this big week.

HALSY

(*Voice over*)
Here's where the factory scout signs star material

Waiting for HALSY, RITA breast-feeds her infant in the front seat of the pickup.

HALSY

(*Voice over*)
Here's where the Cuban whore knows her venereal

Looking for one person in particular, HALSY moves through a swelter of riders, mechanics and sponsors.

HALSY

(*Voice over*)
Here's where the beardown boys bump the best horse

HALSY climbs toward the top of the grandstands. He looks down and surveys the entire raceway.

HALSY

(*Voice over*)
For here is America's number-one course.

Far in the distance HALSY sees what he's been looking for: a tiny figure methodically walking the track.

Track

Cut to LITTLE walking the track and mumbling seriously to himself as he studies the pavement.

He stops and squints more closely at the ground. He picks up a small bolt and throws it aside. He continues on, mumbling.

144

Grandstands

HALSY smiles, proud to see LITTLE has made it this far.

He almost dances down the many steps and at the bottom gives one last look after LITTLE before he turns in whichever direction the pickup is parked.

Track

LITTLE continues on around the track, studying every inch and discoursing with himself.

He walks as high as he can on the steep concrete banks that make Daytona famous.

Pickup Interior

HALSY gets in behind the wheel but can't start the car right away because RITA, standing in the passenger door, is changing the baby's diapers on her side of the front seat.

> RITA
>
> Is he here?

> HALSY
>
> Who?

He looks down at the baby for a moment and then ahead, as though suppressing impatience.

> RITA
>
> You're not looking for any trouble, are you?

> HALSY
>
> Look-it, all's I'm looking for out of this is a factory contract.

He sighs. He'd like to get moving. RITA tries to hurry.

> HALSY
>
> I'm just tired of leaning on dealers all over the country to ride their brands at every fairgrounds and country fair all over the country.

RITA gets in and has hardly closed the door before he starts the motor.

> HALSY
>
> Just getting on some factory team at forty or sixty thousand a year, that's all Daytona means to me.

RITA must hold her baby protectively as the car jolts forward and twists through the heavy traffic. She looks uneasily at HALSY.

Telephone Booth

RITA carries her baby on one hip as she dials. It is night and this booth is on the grounds of a flashy motel on Motel Row, Daytona.

> RITA
>
> (*Into phone*) Ah, yeah hello. Yeah, Miami Beach information? (*Then:*) Yeah, I'd like is there a Fontomblow Hotel or something? Yeah, right. Fontomblow. (*They give her the number.*) How much to call from here? Daytona Beach.

The operator tells her and RITA counts her change, shifting the baby to her other hip.

RITA

(*Into phone*) Yeah, okay.

She puts the change in and while she waits she shifts the baby back again, tired and apprehensive.

RITA

(*Into phone*) Yeah, ah . . . listen, is, ah . . . do you have some people there named, ah . . . Mr. and Mrs. Leopold Nebraska? (*Then:*) Yes, please. (*Who's calling?*) Rita. (*We must know who's calling.*) Rita.

In a moment one hears an anxious female hello. But RITA has lost her nerve. The hello continues with growing anxiety, abetted by unclear asides. RITA says nothing. Finally another voice comes on and continues to plead: "Darling please, this is Daddy." Unable to respond, RITA slowly hangs up.

Parking Area

Babe in arms, RITA thoughtfully crosses the motel parking area.

At the door to her room she pauses as though having to come to some resolve.

Motel Room

Four or five racers, among them HALSY, sit around a table, playing poker. They are drinking beer and are all a little tight, particularly HALSY. They look up nervously as RITA enters.

Hell, I thought we were being raided.

The game proceeds and RITA with her baby crosses wearily to the bed.

DEALER

Is poker legal in Florida or what?

HALSY

Anything goes you can get away with, I always say. (*To* RITA) Did you lock the door?

RITA puts the baby down and crosses back to the door. Clearly she wishes the game would end and the company leave.

RITA

Children neglect is not legal anywhere, Halsy.

HALSY

Hell, what do you want me to do? They're into me ten bucks.

Before RITA can lock the door, it opens and four more riders come in, among them LITTLE.

NEW RIDER

Okay, you guys, this is a raid.

LITTLE and RITA are suddenly, unexpectedly face to face and both turn immediately to HALSY under the lamp at the card table.

HALSY

Well, if it's not Little Fauss, my old Contralto tuner? Good deal.

And he gets up and shakes LITTLE's hand in an expansiveness that is equal parts vulnerable and vicious.

LITTLE

How you doing, Halsy?

HALSY

Fine time for a raid. They're into me ten bucks.

POKER PLAYER

Who's into who?

HALSY

Somebody's into somebody. You want a beer? You know Rita, don't you? Oh yeah, that's right. And our kid, you ain't seen our kid.

He gestures to the bundle on the bed and sways between the forces of tension and booze. LITTLE, equally uneasy, shuffles around as though warned there's a cobra in the room.

LITTLE

Looks like a good baby.

HALSY

Oh yeah, there's nothing like a kid. Nothing in the world like a kid to . . .

POKER PLAYER

You in, Halsy?

HALSY

Yeah, great, put me in. (*To* LITTLE) You want a beer?

LITTLE

Well, I just came in for a minute so I think I'll just go.

HALSY

So you're staying at cockroach manor too. That's what I call this place . . . cockroach manor.

LITTLE

Ritzy enough for me.

HALSY

Oh sure, it's a beautiful place. I was only kidding. No, it's a beautiful place . . . TV . . .

DEALER

You playing cards, Knox, or not?

HALSY

You're only in Florida once, I always say and . . . all my friends are here.

He gestures to the backs of all his friends as they surround the card table. There is a significant if unintentional pause. It is up to the one friend that matters to make the next move.

LITTLE

Well, I better get some sleep if I want to get some practice laps in tomorrow.

HALSY

(*Taking this as the final rejection*) Yeah, you better get some sleep.

And he rejoins the card game, which had in fact gone on without him. He grabs up the cards to deal. It is not his turn. But no one objects, as his mood is clearly too combustible.

HALSY

Me, I do my partying before I race. Then I'm

so hung over, all's I want to do is get that damn race over. Damn if I don't race better just trying to get that damn race over and back on the road.

LITTLE

(*Who would like to be conciliatory if he could find the way.*) Looking for another Denny's down the road, right?

HALSY

(*Not recognizing the white flag*) So you better get your sleep, Little, and say your prayers you stay erect for Sunday for that Two Hundred Miler.

LITTLE

Me? You're the one ought to say your prayers. You're the one can't stay erect.

HALSY

What are you talking about, man, you can't stay erect five minutes.

LITTLE

On the turns, I mean. Around the turns.

HALSY

That's what I mean. What do you mean?

Everyone else has just tuned out this naked, clumsy confrontation and waits suspended for the air to clear.

HALSY pushes his cards forward, scrambling them with the others.

HALSY

It's not my deal. Whose deal is it? Hell, you guys know what time it is. I'm not running a casino in here, damnit.

He gets up and heads for the bathroom, gesturing to the bed and the baby as he passes.

HALSY

When's this kid supposed to get any sleep?

He goes into the bathroom and slams the door.

The riders shrug and shuffle and depart.

LITTLE is alone with RITA. He is at the door but he doesn't want to leave, as at no time during the scene did he really want to leave.

LITTLE

How are you, Rita?

RITA

I'm fine, Little. How are you?

LITTLE

I'm fine.

RITA

Good.

LITTLE

Only the draft board's got me.

HALSY comes out of the bathroom in his shorts.

HALSY

Thought you had to go home and go to sleep, Little.

LITTLE

(*Lonely and fearful and needing a friend*) I got drafted, Halsy. The draft board's got me.

HALSY stands over the baby between the twin beds.

HALSY

Is she going to sleep here tonight or here?

RITA

(*Coldly*) She'll sleep with me.

HALSY shrugs and pulls back the covers on the free bed.

HALSY

(*In response to* LITTLE) Crash your bike on Sunday and get reclassified. That's what I'd do.

He gets into bed.

LITTLE

You mean unload on purpose and hurt myself?

HALSY

That's what I done.

LITTLE

Well, I don't feature that.

HALSY lies on his stomach and is already almost asleep.

HALSY

Only thing is when you go to wreck yourself a little you usually wreck yourself a lot.

LITTLE shakes his head in well-meant disbelief, but RITA looks down at HALSY's scar and wonders if at last she's heard the truth.

Raceway

HALSY pulls his beat-up pickup past what seems miles of sleek new Volkswagen buses and uniformed factory teams of riders and mechanics.

When he finally finds a place to park, he all but falls
out of the driver's seat, so hung over is he. He wears a
gaucho hat.

HALSY

> (*Cursing to himself*) Park any farther away and I'd
> have to ask Fidel Castro!

He holds his head and sways and looks out to the track,
where practice laps are already in progress.

Track

Although it is early, LITTLE and others are roaring down
the track.

Stands

RITA, carrying baby, back rest, basinette, thermos, books,
sun reflector, umbrella, portable radio and a small suitcase
of fresh diapers and baby food, finds a place alone, halfway up in the stands peopled by wives and children.
She sets up and arranges her paraphernalia as the practice
laps groan before her.

Track

Continue with a mumbling LITTLE as he takes a final lap
along the great big-time Daytona.

Pits

HALSY has changed into his leathers and got his bike off
the pickup and is getting ready for practice when LITTLE
glides in.

Looks like you got yourself some cycle there.

HALSY looks up sickly and then continues to work on his bike, which is indeed new and flashy.

HALSY

(*Slow to respond*) Right about one thing, Little. Not to sidehack with me anyway.

LITTLE

Yeah, I heard old Wally Jay was fool enough to climb on with you.

HALSY gives him a dark look and then, pushing his bike, starts toward the line of racers waiting to use the track. LITTLE follows.

As they cross the pits:

LITTLE

Must of done pretty good, you teaming up with Wally, to show up at Daytona with a Taco Naomi looks like brang-new.

HALSY continues in sick silence for a while. Then:

HALSY

Me and Wally Jay went down in San Jose, Little, I guess you didn't hear. I damn near lost my ass and Wally Jay got himself killed.

Line

HALSY joins the line almost at the start, a privilege he's entitled to since he has not yet been out this morning. LITTLE comes in beside him, without this privilege, yet wanting to say something consoling about Wally Jay; he can only clear his throat, however, a sympathy lost in the din.

HALSY

(*Shouting after a moment*) So what I done was I started a fund in his memorial and rose eight hundred bucks. That's how come I got a Taco Naomi. So as Old Wally's memory could live on.

He moves up in line. LITTLE remains paralyzed as the above remarks sink in.

HALSY looks back. He removes his gaucho hat and hands it to LITTLE as though to say: If you're not going to practice, take care of this for me. He puts on his hairnet and then his helmet and moves forward again.

An official motions HALSY onto the track, and LITTLE watches the Taco Naomi roar into action. Only then does he move. He tosses HALSY's hat into the dirt and revs his bike forward, not waiting for a signal from the official and in fact ignoring the official's angry gestures to stop. He grinds out onto the track after HALSY.

Race

LITTLE and HALSY alone on the Daytona Speedway for several laps.

As they roar down the front straight to start-finish, *cut to:*

Stands

RITA bathes her face in the hot light of her sun reflector and listens to her portable radio, stonily aloof to LITTLE

156

and HALSY, who almost as one shoot down the straight before her.

Motel Room

It is late at night and RITA in the darkened room stares at a silent television set which casts her face in eerie shadows.

HALSY
(*From the bed*) I'm not asleep.

RITA
I know. I got your vibrations.

HALSY
(*Not satisfied*) That's right, you get vibrations.

RITA
(*Unmoving*) I could adjust very easily to being blind.

HALSY
What are you trying to do, go blind with that thing?

RITA
Shouldn't you go to sleep, Halsy?

HALSY
Rita?

RITA
(*Negative.*) Tomorrow's the big day.

HALSY
(*Saying it*) You'll never hear me say I love you.

157

RITA's eyes don't leave the silent moving pictures of the TV.

> RITA
>
> That's okay.

> HALSY
>
> Not since Bunny Patchen, nobody's ever heard me say I love them.

> RITA
>
> (*Relieved, resolved*) I understand.

> HALSY
>
> It's just this rule I have.

He stares through the darkness at her immobile face in the dead light of the silent screen.

> HALSY
>
> (*Hardly aloud*) But I do.

Motel Exterior

It is the following morning and LITTLE is posing his bike in the open doorway of his motel room. He has the camera once stolen by HALSY and as he steps back to take this picture a MAN from a neighboring room appears in his bathrobe, walking an infinitesimal dog.

> MAN
>
> Looks like some pretty jazzy equipment you got there.

> LITTLE
>
> Yeah well, in my line you got to have the best.

158

MAN

That's what I thought. Professional.

LITTLE

Tch. Damn equipment gives me away every time.

MAN

(*Wanting to be known as a rake, so talking out of the side of his mouth*) Well, you see a photographer around a motel, you want to be sure you're not on candid camera, if you know what I mean. (*Rolling his eyes proudly*) This is not my wife's dog!

Another Angle

As LITTLE pushes his bike toward his truck, we see the parking area of the motel crowded with riders, their teams and families, loading up cars and campers.

LITTLE

No, I'm with *Life*.

MAN

Life?

LITTLE

Well, *Cycle Life* is what it's called, in so many words.

MAN

I thought you meant *Life* magazine. I was going to *say*.

But LITTLE's attention is suddenly drawn to the center of the parking area, where HALSY stands in his undershorts, squinting around confusedly.

Parking Area

In the background, HALSY gets some startled looks but he is too dazed to be aware of them. LITTLE approaches.

HALSY

(*Bereft*) She's gone.

LITTLE

Who's gone?

HALSY

Who the hell do you think's gone, man. Rita.

LITTLE

She's not with me.

HALSY

She's split.

LITTLE

Don't look at me.

HALSY

I know she's not with you. What would she want with you, you gimp? She just cut out.

LITTLE

(*After a moment*) Where would she go?

HALSY

I don't know, screw her. Where did she come from? (*Sniffs.*) You going to eat any breakfast?

He nervously surveys the whole motel complex one final time, anguished tears just beneath the surface. Then hurt but hearty:

HALSY

They got any Denny's down here? Let's eat.

Restaurant

It is jammed with riders, their tuners, their sponsors, their families and some of the minor multitude Daytona draws.

HALSY and LITTLE are halfway through a meal in this clatter. HALSY holds himself together with anger, but LITTLE has gone dismal and limp.

> HALSY
> (*Mouthful.*) I turned down Taco Naomi, did I tell you?

> LITTLE
> Good for you.

> HALSY
> I told them they could shove their contract. Nobody runs my life like that.

> LITTLE
> Where to go, where to be, what time.

> HALSY
> Sponsorship's nowhere, man. It's all politics.

> LITTLE
> (*Forlorn*) No one would ever run my life like that.

> HALSY
> I had a couple offers to race Europe, which is what I'll probably do.

> LITTLE
> (*Sighing*) Actually, what my plans are just now is just to stay drunk until they induck me.

HALSY

(*Mouthful.*) I'd head for the fence and get re-classified. What time is it?

HALSY hurriedly finishes up what LITTLE leaves and then they both move through the throng to the door.

Restaurant Exterior

Coming out into the bright morning sunlight, HALSY inhales more than his share of Florida in a forced buoyancy LITTLE is unable to imitate.

LITTLE

What a day to go on.

HALSY

(*Emotion somewhere, but repressed.*) Oh no. If a chick's going to go, she's going to go on your birthday or Christmas Eve. They got their timing down. They know just when to cut you.

LITTLE

Let's race.

As they cross the parking area to their cars, HALSY puts an arm briefly around LITTLE's shoulders.

HALSY

Daytona, man. We made Daytona anyway, didn't we?

LITTLE

Not yet.

They stop at their cars.

It's not how you do, Little. It's where you been. Ain't you learned that yet?

It's how you do, Hals.

They look at each other and smirk at their differences; large as they are, their similarities outweigh them. HALSY climbs into his pickup. LITTLE climbs into his truck. Before they drive out of the parking lot, each leans to his window and gives the other a thumbs-up sign of good luck.

Daytona

The pickup and the truck travel to the raceway.

Raceway

The pickup and the truck move slowly through thick traffic as they turn onto the speedway grounds.

The avenue to the pits is choked with vehicles.

In the pits, what seems like hundreds of bikes are being unloaded from trucks, trailers and pickups.

Even this early, the stands are filling up.

The pits are busier and better run than we have seen them heretofore at lesser events.

Officials cluster, as serious as surgical teams.

Teams of contracted riders, wearing uniform leathers and otherwise rather stamped out, huddle together,

163

slightly aloof from their nonetheless sacred, glittering bikes.

The stands are jammed now. The excitement there and in the pits is momentous and legitimate.

Nearly a hundred bikes move into position at start-finish.

The flag down, these bikes send up a deafening roar and compress into one oddly lethargic mass that digs in and throws back the enormous straightaway.

Somewhere is HALSY, somewhere is LITTLE, but they are lost in the crowd for they are not winners but rather among those who make no significant mark and leave no permanent trace.